I0061566

THE DELIVERY GAP

This compelling book lays bare the systemic problems that have plagued major government projects for too long. With precision and candour, Simcock unravels the real reasons for repeated failures and presents a roadmap for meaningful reform. This book is an urgent call to action for ministers, policymakers, civil servants and anyone invested in effective governance. A must-read for those who believe we can – and must – do better.

—Francis Maude (Lord Maude of Horsham),
Former Cabinet Office Minister

A refreshingly clear perspective on eight mega public sector projects, and why they did not deliver according to plan. It is one man's perspective, but from a man who has been in central positions in the government projects ecosystem since 2007. His narrative offers real insight into the reasons for failure, and he draws equally refreshing recommendations to improve future mega projects. For anyone involved in, or concerned with Government delivery, this short book offers a clear and concise perspective on how to improve things.

—Sir John A. Manzoni,
Former Chief Executive of the Civil Service

This highly readable work draws on many different perspectives to set out why so many major Government projects are destined to fail. It is essential reading for everyone who wants to see better delivery: and that's all of us!

—Rt Hon Sir Jeremy Quin,
Former Defence and Cabinet Office Minister

The Delivery Gap is a great contribution to one of the most important questions of our time. Why do public sector programmes often get into difficulty? Essential reading for anyone involved with the planning or execution of large projects.

—Mark Wild,
CEO of HS2 Ltd, former CEO of Crossrail Ltd

If you are about to take on a key management or leadership role in delivering a complex programme, read this book. Jonathan Simcock is one of the most experienced programme delivery professionals in the country, leading some of the largest programmes in the public and private sectors. His succinct and penetrating insights into why major programmes fail will have some uncomfortable resonance for those who have been at the sharp end and have the scars to show.

The conclusions and recommendations are easy to understand and seemingly obvious, but why are they not recognised? Perhaps this will present the reader with some, uncomfortable dilemmas to address in their work going forward, but also an opportunity to act.

—*Sir Simon Bollom*,
Former CEO of Defence Equipment and Support,
Ministry of Defence

This book raises important issues about a long history of unsuccessful delivery of many major Government projects, and the author's experience brings valuable perspectives to the underlying reasons.

—*David Goldstone CBE*,
Former CEO of Restoration & Renewal Delivery Authority

A brave but insightful book that has grasped the essence of the challenges! Let's hope that the author's efforts and the themes from this book can influence how we improve things to deliver the economic growth that we so desperately need from Government projects.

—*Mark Thurston*,
CEO Anglian Water and former CEO of HS2 Ltd

Through his own deep experience of capital projects in both the private and public sectors, Jonathan Simcock has produced a work of great insight into the many challenges of delivering major projects in a government setting. His recipe for improving outcomes should become mandatory reading for all involved.

—*Tony Meggs*,
Former CEO of the Infrastructure and Projects Authority

THE DELIVERY GAP

Why Government Projects Really Fail and What Can Be Done About It

BY

JONATHAN SIMCOCK

Former Executive Director, Major Projects Directorate of the Office of Government Commerce, UK

emerald
PUBLISHING

United Kingdom – North America – Japan – India
Malaysia – China

Emerald Publishing Limited
Emerald Publishing, Floor 5, Northspring, 21-23 Wellington Street,
Leeds LS1 4DL.

First edition 2025

Copyright © 2025 Jonathan Simcock.
Published under exclusive licence by Emerald Publishing Limited.

Reprints and permissions service
Contact: www.copyright.com

No part of this book may be reproduced, stored in a retrieval system,
transmitted in any form or by any means electronic, mechanical,
photocopying, recording or otherwise without either the prior written
permission of the publisher or a licence permitting restricted copying
issued in the UK by The Copyright Licensing Agency and in the USA
by The Copyright Clearance Center. No responsibility is accepted
for the accuracy of information contained in the text, illustrations
or advertisements. The opinions expressed in these chapters are not
necessarily those of the Author or the publisher.

British Library Cataloguing in Publication Data
A catalogue record for this book is available from the British Library

ISBN: 978-1-83662-485-1 (Print)
ISBN: 978-1-83662-482-0 (Online)
ISBN: 978-1-83662-484-4 (Epub)

INVESTOR IN PEOPLE

This book is dedicated to the thousands of public servants who have valiantly struggled to deliver huge public sector projects over the last two decades. To rise each morning and strive with energy and hope in the face of systemic headwinds represents an un-sung heroism.

> *It is not the critic who counts: not the man who points out how the strong man stumbles or where the doer of deeds could have done better. The credit belongs to the man who is actually in the arena, whose face is marred by dust and sweat and blood, who strives valiantly, who errs and comes up short again and again, because there is no effort without error or shortcoming, but who knows the great enthusiasms, the great devotions, who spends himself in a worthy cause; who, at the best, knows, in the end, the triumph of high achievement, and who, at the worst, if he fails, at least he fails while daring greatly, so that his place shall never be with those cold and timid souls who knew neither victory nor defeat.*

—Theodore Roosevelt[1]
(With apologies for Teddy's characteristic sexism.)

---

[1]Theodore Roosevelt. Speech at the Sorbonne, Paris. 23 April 1910.

CONTENTS

PREFACE

Some of what government achieves is accomplished through policy. A tweak to taxation, reform of the curriculum, funding more policemen. But sometimes government has to actually build or buy something. A road, a hospital, a school, a defence system. And sometimes it has to do something big. Really big. A fleet of nuclear submarines, a completely secure data infrastructure linking every home in the country with every energy company, the first new underground railway across London for 40 years, an IT system big enough for the health records of every person in the country. The private sector plays its part, but only government can lead projects on this scale. The problem is that if you compare what these mega-projects actually deliver with what was originally intended, successive UK Governments have a really miserable record. Almost universally, very big projects are either late, over budget, deliver less than promised – or all three. Some, like HS2, are never completed at all.

And it really matters. The UK is emerging from political turbulence and the Covid pandemic deep in debt, with stagnant growth, poor productivity, and taxation levels at historic highs. We do not have tens of billions of pounds to waste on half a high-speed railway. Our degraded public services need reform now, not after years lost to failed IT projects. The world has become a more dangerous place; national security requires new capabilities to arrive on time. And the climate challenge can't be met without unprecedented transformation in the nation's energy systems.

From outside the opaque world of public sector project delivery, commentators struggle to understand why our performance is so poor. How hard can it be? Surely you just decide what to do, work out how long it will take and how much it will cost, then procure somebody to deliver it. Not everything will be easy, to be sure, but surely we should be successful far more often than we are.

In the wake of the cancellation of HS2, I set out to understand what is causing this malaise. I spoke to the insiders – ex-ministers, advisors, civil servants and project managers – who have tried, and mostly failed, to deliver some of the largest and most complex projects of the last two decades. Through their stories, I began to understand the structures and incentives that are at the root of failure. In the course of these conversations, I realised that most of my preconceptions about what has to change were wrong. I now believe that no amount of improved process, enhanced capability, or sharpened accountabilities will solve the problem, unless the destructive underlying tendencies described in this book are exposed and addressed.

Just to be clear. I am not saying that no public sector project is ever successful. Some are. Or that no other country struggles with the same issues. They do. But I am saying that we can and must do better. If we are to overcome the huge challenges we face as a country – poor productivity, high debt, low growth, rising security threats and a changing climate, we must change the way we think about mega-projects. We have to close the delivery gap.

ACKNOWLEDGEMENTS

I am enormously grateful to the past and present ministers, senior officials and delivery leaders who have shared their experiences so openly with me in the research for this book. I have named them when I could, but even when their contributions have been anonymised, I have strived to retain the essence of their insights. If there is any wisdom in what follows, most of it comes from them. Where there are errors, they are all my own.

1

DEATH OF A PROJECT: HS2

You know that feeling you get when you hear about the death of a long-sick relative? It isn't unexpected. But somehow it is still a shock. There had been speculation for weeks that Prime Minister Rishi Sunak would make an announcement about the future of the HS2 project in his 2023 party conference speech:

> *If we are to create change and drive growth across our country, then we must get our infrastructure right. A false consensus has taken root that all that matters are links between our big conurbations. It said that the most important connection those cities could have was to London, and not anywhere else. And it said that the only links that mattered were north to south: not east to west. HS2 is the ultimate example of the old consensus. The result is a project whose costs have more than doubled, which has been repeatedly delayed and it is not scheduled to reach here in Manchester for almost two decades...and for which the economic case has massively weakened with the changes to business travel post Covid. I say, to those who backed the project in the first place, the facts have changed. And the right thing to do when the facts change, is to have the courage to change direction. And so, I am ending this long-running saga. I am cancelling the rest of the HS2 project.[1]*

To me, it felt like proof that I was living in 'can't do' Britain. After more than a decade of development, with billions already spent, was the biggest infrastructure project in the post-war period really being stopped in its tracks half-way through its first phase? And on a political whim?

My first thought was for my brother David, whose family had been uprooted from their home of 30 years, the home he expected to grow old in, because it was on the high-speed route between Birmingham and Crewe – a section of the line which would now, it appeared, never be built. He had seen the small country community in which he lived destroyed as some had their homes compulsorily purchased against their will and others reluctantly sold to the government to avoid many years of construction stress and permanent loss of peace and quiet. Returning recently to the village, he had seen most of the cottages empty and over-grown or else let to short-term tenants. Weeds choked the pond around which the community had dwelt.

Over the years, even as he wrestled with the heartless process of assessment, valuation and revaluation of his home, my brother had always been phlegmatic about the reality that infrastructure projects have losers as well as winners. 'You can't build a railway without disturbing anyone.' But now there would be no railway. Thousands of lives had been dislocated and dozens of communities blighted for nothing.

My next thought was for the hundreds of professionals I had met over the years who had devoted a chunk of their careers to this one great national endeavour: The civil servants, consultants, engineers, project managers, lawyers, commercial professionals, and contractors lured by a once in a generation challenge. Despite the announcement, some of them would still have many years of HS2 work ahead of them. Phase One was still years from completion. There were tunnels to finish, track to lay, and stations to build. The signalling contract had not even been let. Some of them would be busier than ever. Contracts would have to be terminated or renegotiated. £600 million worth of now superfluous land and property, including David's, would have to be sold off.[2] And HS2 Ltd, the government owned company which had taken years to develop, would have to be wound down and then wound up. Abandoning HS2 would keep hundreds of people busy for years. But it wouldn't be fun. I knew from my own experience how quickly a driven, energetic, project organisation can be infested by collective disillusionment. The fog of failure drifts into every meeting room. Good people begin looking for escape routes. Less good people look for somewhere to hide. Who would join this miserable endeavour if they had an alternative without the cloud of failure hanging over it? How on earth, I wondered, would they motivate the tens of thousands of people already working on the project to stay, and attract the others they would need to bring at least Phase One of the project to a successful conclusion?

But in the months after Rishi Sunak's announcement, it became clear that there could be no successful conclusion to Phase One. The National Audit Office catalogued the dismal consequences of the Prime Minister's decision.[3]

With no affordable scheme for an HS2 station at Euston, the trains seemed destined to terminate at Old Oak Common, seven miles further out of London. Platforms at Birmingham Curzon Street would be built, but never made operational, because not building them would be more expensive than carrying on. And north of Birmingham, HS2 trains running onto the West Coast Main Line would have fewer seats and run slower than the services they replaced. Capacity between Manchester and Birmingham would actually reduce, so passengers would have to be discouraged from travelling by rail at busy times. Phase One of HS2 in isolation is a railway that nobody would ever have dreamt of building. The Department for Transport's own economic assessment is that the benefit will never outweigh the costs. The London to Birmingham leg only ever made sense in the context of completing the northern phases.

If Sunak was trying, a year out from a general election, to show himself to be a bold and decisive leader ready to make tough decisions for the greater good, then it didn't work. To most commentators it seemed to be an act of vandalism committed against the legacy of his own party's 13 years in power. Perhaps I would not have found the death of HS2 so dispiriting if it had really just been this – the desperate political act of an unpopular Prime Minister. But in truth, the HS2 project had struggled from the start.

*

Since the completion of High Speed One, the line from London to the Channel Tunnel, there had been little serious interest in high-speed rail for the UK before 2008. A study commissioned by the Department for Transport in 2005 concluded that high-speed rail would never be the best use of limited resources.[4] UK cities are too close together to warrant the cost of very high-speed trains. More conventional projects would always offer better value for money. But after Ruth Kelly, the Labour Transport Secretary, resigned during the 2008 Labour Party conference to spend more time with her family, the Conservative opposition saw an opportunity to kill a number of birds with one stone. By announcing that in government they would scrap the expansion of Heathrow airport and instead spend £20 billion on a completely new high-speed railway, they could burnish David Cameron's green credentials, kill off a project unpopular with their South of England constituents (not to mention their noisy London Mayor Boris Johnson), and paint the Labour government as unimaginative, disorganised and out of touch, all at the same time. Their new project would serve the apparently never-ending growth in north-south rail passenger numbers by connecting the existing high-speed link between London and Paris with a new railway to the North. Passengers from Birmingham, Manchester and Leeds would reach London in 45, 80 and 97 minutes respectively. Manchester to Leeds would take 17 minutes. And those who needed an airport could use a new high-speed connection to Heathrow. The project would be funded by a combination of public and private sector finance, and services would begin operating in 2027.[5] In contrast to Labour's uninspiring commitment to another runway at Heathrow, it sounded new and exciting.

Two Labour Secretaries of State later, the concept had become bipartisan. Labour Transport Secretary Andrew Adonis's White

Paper, 'High Speed Rail', landed in Parliament in the months leading up to the 2010 election. It promised to bring Britain in line with
the nations already enjoying the thrill of high velocity.

> Not only France's TGV and the pioneering Japanese
> Shinkansen but new high speed networks across Europe
> and Asia are increasing capacity, slashing travel times,
> transforming the connections between cities, and offering
> the most comfortable and convenient travelling experi-
> ence in history.

For a project that was still years away from the drawing board,
the scheme was remarkably specific. There was to be a Y-shaped
network of lines from London to Birmingham, and then north
to Manchester, and north-east to the east midlands, Sheffield and
Leeds. The trains would travel at 250 miles per hour. A journey
from Birmingham to Canary Wharf would take just 70 minutes,
and from Leeds to Canary Wharf a hundred minutes. There would
be a phased opening from 2026. The cost of the whole scheme
would be £30 billion.[6]

After the general election brought the Conservatives to power
in coalition with the Liberal Democrats, the incoming administration caught the hospital pass. The new Transport Secretary, Philip
Hammond, was told by David Cameron to 'Get HS2 done. Get
out there and promote it like mad, get it done, get it through,
that's your only task.'[7] A bill for the London to Birmingham leg of
the railway was introduced to Parliament in 2013. Despite being
government policy, the whole project was far from popular in
the Conservative party. The bill took over three years to receive
Royal Assent as every vested interest tried to influence the scope
in one direction or another. A Cabinet member of the time told
me about an informal backbench group which would 'get the HS2
project people in to shout at them about this particularly beautiful grave or listed building or Civil War battlefield site'. Another
minister told me, 'David Cameron ended up committing to things
that cost more than he was putting into the entire broadband roll-
out across the United Kingdom.' A totemic example is the kilometre-
long structure in Buckinghamshire being built to protect bats

from the trains.[8] As the project progressed and the scope evolved, so did the costs. By the time Prime Minister Boris Johnson was faced with the final decision about whether to proceed – at least with the first phase from London to Birmingham – the costs for the full Y-shaped scheme had grown to over £100 billion and it wouldn't open until the late 2030s. With costs up and benefits delayed, the economics of the project were much less attractive than the picture painted by Adonis a decade earlier. So Johnson commissioned an old associate, Doug Oakervee, the man who had championed the Crossrail Project for him when he was London Mayor, to do a final review. Oakervee's conclusion was that the project should proceed, but only if subsequent phases were also approved as part of an 'integrated plan for the GB rail network',[9] and on the precondition that costs were reduced by cutting the maximum train speed, limiting the number of trains per hour, and renegotiating the major civil contracts which were by now nearing the point of signature. The Prime Minister accepted Oakervee's conclusion, but not his preconditions. Phase One was to proceed with a funding limit of £40 billion. Johnson insisted that building the full Y scheme remained government policy, but in fact resources working on the eastern leg to Leeds had already been diverted onto the Birmingham to Crewe, and Crewe to Manchester sections.

The Department for Transport issued HS2 Ltd with a Notice to Proceed, allowing the construction proper to begin. But the £40 billion figure was based on very immature design work. And the huge civil contracts prioritised schedule over costs in a way that incentivised getting shovels in the ground before the design was bedded down. Evolution of the design and concessions made to planning authorities led to recycling and rework. By 2024, the projected cost of Phase One had grown to £49–57 billion, up to 45% more than the budget set in 2020.[10] And that excluded the impact of post-pandemic inflation. HS2 was destined to fail.

So my dejection at the death of HS2 was not simply distress at the decision. The fate of this railway amplified an unacknowledged notion that was already resonating in my head. A growing feeling that failure of huge government projects is somehow predestined. Even worse than this depressing idea was my feeling of complicity. Hadn't I had been part of this problem since my first encounter with the world of government projects when I first entered Trevelyan House on Great Peter Street in Westminster on a drizzly July day in 2007?

2

THE DELIVERY GAP

It's the Indonesian Embassy now, but in 2007 Trevelyan House was the headquarters of the Office of Government Commerce, a little-known enclave in the most powerful department of government – Her Majesty's Treasury. I'd been recruited to make the biggest government projects more successful.

The building's current use is ironic because I had once spent a few days in government offices in Jakarta, and I knew more about what went on in the government in Indonesia than I did about Whitehall. I was spectacularly unqualified. I had no experience of government projects at all. I was recruited because no civil servant at the right grade had applied. The Office of Government Commerce had been created in 2000 by the Blair government on the recommendation of Sir Peter Gershon, then a main board director of the defence contractor GEC Marconi. Gershon recommended a single centre of excellence for procurement and the management of large complex projects. He was recruited as its first Chief Executive, reporting jointly to the Prime Minister and Chancellor. But Gershon had moved on in 2004 and his successor, a civil service insider, lacked Gershon's clout and credibility. Three years on, the Office of Government Commerce was no longer seen as the place to be for up-and-coming public sector talent. So, lacking internal candidates, they recruited me to lead the Major Projects Directorate.

There was a lot going on. A month earlier, Gordon Brown had finally become Prime Minister and he was now enjoying a brief bounce in the polls. The rain I had dodged on Great Peter Street on my first day had been much worse in the South West of England, leading to extensive floods. Brown was photographed commanding the response in his wellingtons, while the leader of the opposition David Cameron was lambasted for leaving the country despite flooding in his Oxfordshire constituency. But Brown's honeymoon was short. Amongst Labour's other problems, the reality was that, after 10 years in power, the tired government was struggling to deliver of a large portfolio of major projects.

Blair's modernisation reforms had led to a slew of projects for rewiring public services. The obsession with fixing the state through huge IT projects had taken hold particularly strongly in the Home Office. After the 9/11 attacks on the World Trade Centre, a scheme to introduce identity cards was developed. Then, when schoolgirls Holly Wells and Jessica Chapman were murdered by their school caretaker in 2003, a Vetting and Barring Programme was started to register everyone who wanted to work with children and block them if they posed a risk. And now the Home Office was preparing to sign a deal with a consortium led by US Defence firm Raytheon to digitise border controls to prevent illegal immigration and to reduce organised crime and terrorism. Every threat to you or your family could be reduced by new IT systems. But the largest of all the IT projects was in Health. The NHS was five years into a huge top-down digitisation of healthcare known as the National Programme. The plan was to improve the quality of patient care while reducing costs by bringing information technology into the 21st century. In the NHS, they described it as the only IT project in the world that could be seen from space.

It wasn't all about IT. The first of a new class of nuclear submarines had just been formally named HMS *Astute* by the Duchess of Cornwall and was 12 months away from its target handover date to the Royal Navy. And two, so far nameless, aircraft carriers were on the drawing board and were expected to enter service in 2014 and 2016. A Joint Strike Fighter Programme was underway to buy the aircraft to fly from them. The department responsible for energy policy was about to launch a competition through which industry could bid for public money to design, construct and operate the UK's first commercial-scale carbon capture and storage demonstration project at a coal-fired power station. Through the recently created Nuclear Decommissioning Authority, the same department was inviting the private sector to bid to decommission the country's nuclear waste sites, including the largest and most hazardous – Sellafield in West Cumbria. Meanwhile, the Department for Transport was dusting down a longstanding idea for Crossrail, a high-capacity underground railway across London. And the Whitehall department with the least institutional capability for delivering major projects had been handed the highest-profile challenge of all. The Department for Culture Media and Sport, whose biggest projects normally involved refurbishing museum buildings, found itself overseeing the multi-billion-pound preparation for the 2012 London Olympics.

These projects were just the very expensive tip of a huge iceberg of smaller projects in every department of state: new schools, new prisons, new hospitals, upgraded roads, and countless IT systems for everything from paying the new Employment Support Allowance and steering offenders through the criminal justice system to making EU payments to farmers.

I had spent my working life in the oil industry, a sector which has its own share of major projects and has had, to say the least, its own share of problems. But I was awed by the scale and risk of what I found in the UK government. And I was stunned to find that virtually all the projects that had been going for any length of time were struggling one way or another. For many, successful delivery seemed seriously in doubt.

What could I do, sitting at the heart of government, in what was now Alistair Darling's Treasury, to help to make these projects succeed? Honestly? Not much. My team changed the way government projects were reviewed through their lifetimes. We staffed a new Major Projects Review Group to scrutinise the biggest projects before they got the green light from Treasury ministers. We developed a process called Starting Gate to test the viability of a project before it started, in an attempt to make sure that only feasible projects would get off the ground. And we introduced the first regular cross-government reporting of project status on the largest and riskiest projects. Every quarter, a report on the largest projects went off to the offices of the Prime Minister and the Chancellor of the Exchequer. To be honest, there was never much evidence that either Brown or Darling ever actually got to see them.

I left the Office of Government Commerce before the end of 2009. Six months later the electorate put the weary Labour administration out of its misery, and David Cameron, George Osborne and Nick Clegg took over. They put Tory grandee Francis Maude in charge of reforming the way central government spent its money, and one of his first actions was to dismantle the Office of Government Commerce. He put the Major Projects Directorate into a new Efficiency and Reform Group in the Cabinet Office. By then, much of government's multi-billion-pound portfolio of mega-projects was in deep trouble. Some of the IT projects were plodding relentlessly on like zombies, without any real spark of life. The Identity Cards, Vetting and Barring, and Electronic Borders programmes were quickly dispatched by the incoming Government. The NHS National Programme rumbled on for another year but was eventually wound up in 2011.

Once they get going, projects delivering physical infrastructure or defence systems are harder to kill than IT projects, even if they are struggling. The aircraft carriers eventually came into service in 2017 and 2019, three years later than planned, and without the aircraft originally anticipated to fly from them. The early Astute class nuclear submarines took much longer and cost much more to get into service than was ever anticipated. But at least some of them did get into service. The energy projects fared worse. The Carbon Capture and Storage programme was cancelled in 2011, relaunched in 2012, cancelled again in 2016 and relaunched again in 2017. Fifteen years on from the original policy, there are still no commercial-scale Carbon Capture and Storage projects in construction in the UK. The contracts for outsourcing management of nuclear decommissioning sites were gradually abandoned between 2016 and 2021 as the Nuclear Decommissioning Authority concluded that the private sector experiment had failed.

In contrast, the Crossrail Project seemed to be going exceptionally well. Since construction got underway at Canary Wharf in 2008, the works made solid progress, first through the main tunnelling phase and then with the installation of the track. Perhaps the country had finally learnt how to deliver massive infra-structure projects. But just four months before the core section of the line was due to open at the end of 2018, problems surfaced publicly. Finishing the stations and completing and testing the train control systems added billions to the cost and years to the project. The full operation of the service was only possible in 2023. By that time, rail passenger numbers nationally were down after Covid-19 and the lack of Crossrail revenues had helped take Transport for London to the brink of financial collapse.

If the record of major projects initiated in the Labour years is poor, the Conservative track record has matched it – particularly for big IT projects. Chief amongst these is the Universal Credit Programme. Iain Duncan Smith brought radical ideas for reform-ing the benefits system to his role as Secretary of State for Work and Pensions. The plan was to bring in-work and out-of-work benefits together into one system in order to make work pay. The required legislation would be passed by 2012 and the whole change would be completed by 2017. The roll-out is still not complete and is now projected for 2029.

Universal Credit was always going to be a controversial project. But even the Tories' lowest-profile projects have become bogged down. What could be less contentious than providing radios for the blue-light services? In 2014, the Home Office announced a pro-ject to replace the existing communication system. The idea was to complete the switch by 2019, before the existing contract was due to expire. From the outset, the programme was beset by commer-cial and technical problems. The end-date was repeatedly extended, eventually to 2026, and even that date now looks unrealistic. As the schedule has drifted, the delivery costs have increased, not to mention the cost of maintaining the existing service long after its original use-by date.

Run from Parliament rather than from Whitehall, but still firmly in the public sector, a project to stop the Palace of Westminster either falling or burning down was conceived as early as 2012. After much sucking of teeth, a joint committee of both Houses was appointed in 2015 to decide how to proceed. Eventually, in 2019, parliamentarians voted to set up an independently governed

delivery authority to run the project. But deciding what the authority is actually to deliver has so far proved impossible. In the same
five-year period another UNESCO heritage site, Notre-Dame, has
burned down and been completely rebuilt.

For a decade and a half after I left the Office of Government
Commerce, I remained on the periphery of many of these projects.
I led project reviews, sat on the Major Projects Review Group, and
for five years I managed a private sector company set up to provide
the infrastructure for yet another multi-billion-pound government
project – the introduction of smart-meters into every domestic
property in the country. Our aim was to have the job essentially
done by 2020. Despite all our best efforts, we missed the target by
a mile, and the government is now aiming to make 80% of proper-
ties smart by the beginning of 2026.

The exception to this apparently universal story of failure was,
of course, the 2012 London Olympics. After an early increase in
the budget, and despite years of doom-laden predictions from the
press, the stadia went up on time and the transport infrastructure
worked. The Games themselves were a triumph. Even a botched
security contract was heroically rescued by the army. Here, finally,
was evidence that Britain could, after all, deliver large complex
projects on time and on budget.

It was in the afterglow of the Olympic success, and bolstered
by the early progress of Crossrail, that HS2 began to gain momentum. In time, its political momentum became unstoppable. And in
February 2020, despite the fault lines of failure already being visible, Phase One was approved. Three and a half years and many
billions of pounds later, the project was cancelled. What is going
on? Why do we have such a poor record in delivering huge government projects? Why is it so difficult?

3

OBFUSCATION AND DELUSION: CROSSRAIL

Rishi Sunak's cancellation of High Speed 2 was a shock but not a surprise. But the other railway project shocker of recent years came, to me at least, completely out of the blue. In August 2018, Crossrail Ltd, the company charged with delivering the largest infrastructure project in Europe, announced that the railway would not now open in November as planned. The announcement was vague about when the Elizabeth Line would actually open, but it looked like the delay would be substantial. It is one thing to find, at some point in the life of a decade-long project, that the original end-date had become unrealistic. But three months before it was due to open? I was stunned. So, apparently, were the project's joint funders, London Mayor Sadiq Khan and Transport Minister, Jo Johnson. A week after the announcement, the Mayor was quizzed by the Chair of the London Assembly.

Mr Mayor, if I can sum this up accurately, you knew just two days before the public at large?

That is correct.[1]

Not only would the railway not open on time, but the project couldn't say with confidence when it would, nor how much more money it would take. Initial hopes that the delay would be less than a year were quickly dashed, and the forecast opening date drifted into 2020. Impacted further by the Covid-19 pandemic, the central underground section eventually opened in May 2022, albeit without one of its main stations. By the end of that year, trains were running on the length of the railway, and a full service, with a final timetable, was operational by May 2023. The additional unbudgeted £4 billion cost, the impact of which was exacerbated by the pandemic's decimation of Transport for London's revenues, became a contentious issue between the Conservative government and the Labour Mayor. A funding deal, which rescued the capital's transport infrastructure from a vicious cycle of 'managed decline', was eventually struck on the fourth anniversary of the Crossrail delay being first revealed.

Ordinary Londoners were affected most. The London Assembly heard from a pregnant woman who worked in central London who had bought a house in Abbey Wood in 2017, in anticipation of the soon-to-arrive Crossrail service. In 2019, with her maternity leave ending, she faced a commute of an hour and 20 minutes each way. 'I now have to navigate getting back to work with finding childcare that opens early enough and closes late enough for me to be able to drop my child off and still make it to work and back on time.' She had to wait for over three more years for the Elizabeth line to reach her.[2]

Other early casualties were the Chair and Chief Executive of Crossrail Ltd. They were replaced by Tony Meggs and Mark Wild. Meggs, the new Chair, was one of my successors as head of central government's efforts to prevent this sort of thing happening. Wild, who became Chief Executive, had been the Managing Director of London Underground. They took control of the project and saw it through, eventually, to completion. When I met Wild in the oak lined library of the Institution of Mechanical Engineers, I asked him what he found when he took over the project, and what was behind the failure to see the problems coming. I was expecting him to provide valuable insights. What I was not expecting was a conversation that felt almost confessional. He explained that for more than two years before the 2018 crash, he had, as well as running London's tube network, also been Transport for London's nominated director on the Crossrail Ltd board. He and Meggs have been rightly feted as the rescuers of Crossrail, but before that, he had also been part of the problem.

> *If I'm brutally honest with you, I can't say my own performance was without blame. I joined the board in September 2016, and by the spring of 2017, I knew that the train was struggling. I also went to Siemens in Germany to review the signalling system, and it became apparent to me we were in quite a bit of trouble. And the physical progress on site, you could see it. So why didn't I say, look, this needs a much stronger intervention? Why did the Infrastructure and Project Authority give it only an amber rating in 2018? Why did the Project Representative write negative reports but not pull the pin? I've got to be honest. I don't think I would let it happen now.*

Since talking to Wild, I have spoken to other insiders and almost all of them have displayed the same level of introspection and contrition. David Hughes was the Chair of the Crossrail Sponsor Board. 'I put my hand up to the failure of the assurance. I need to say that up front. I'm on the list of the guilty.' Most vowed never to let it happen again in their careers. In the course of our conversation, Wild told me an insightful story.

> *I was running Public Transport Victoria in Australia, and I came to London in the spring of 2016 to be interviewed by the Mayor for the job of running London Underground. Well, that morning, the Queen had formally named it the Elizabeth Line. So when I was interviewed by Boris Johnson – he was his usual self – he was absolutely convinced Crossrail would be done on time. But if you look at the photographs ... I'll show you ....*

Wild pulled his iPad from his bag and showed me a photograph of the Queen in the naming ceremony for the Elizabeth Line that spring. It was a great publicity shot. The Queen is unveiling the new purple Elizabeth Line logo in the tunnel at Bond Street. She is surrounded by excited construction workers, engineers and project managers in orange overalls and gleaming white hard-hats. Mark pointed out the beaming Mayor, the Commissioner of Transport for London, and the Chief Executive of Crossrail Ltd. 'But look', he said, 'The station is obviously very incomplete. But that afternoon, he was completely convinced.'

It is a telling story. In retrospect, nobody should have been surprised that the railway was not going to be ready. But the Queen had unveiled the line's new name, and the ribbon-cutting ceremony in 2018 was already in her diary. It became a mantra in the project, whenever the schedule came under question. 'The Queen is booked!'

The August 2018 announcement prompted a number of inquests, all of which pointed to Crossrail Ltd having failed to face up to reality until it became undeniable. These were particularly painful findings for me because, 10 years earlier, when I was still in the Office of Government Commerce, my only contribution to the Crossrail project had been intended to prevent exactly this outcome. The question on the table at that point, as the project neared final approval, was how to free the project team from interference and micromanagement without letting it go rogue. In the world of government projects, you solve this kind of problem through something called 'governance' and there is a small mountain of guidance and advice about it. All it really comes down to is being very clear about three questions. First, who is allowed to make which decisions in the life of the project – about whether to proceed to the next phase or whether to award contracts? Second, how much independent checking should there be of those decisions, and of progress in general? And finally, how is progress to be reported and to whom?

Getting the governance right for Crossrail was complicated because the project was to be jointly funded by the Department for Transport, backed by the Treasury, and the London Mayor through Transport for London. They were both putting up money, and they would both want their interests protected. This always looked tricky, but particularly when the Mayor was from one party and a procession of Transport Secretaries were from another. The chosen solution was that the project would be run at arm's length from both Transport for London and the Department for Transport, in a separate legal entity, Crossrail Ltd, which, while partly funded by central government, would be wholly owned by Transport for

London. In 2008, the two funders signed a contract to this effect. Another contract, between the funders and the company, would set down what the railway had to do. The idea was that Crossrail Ltd would be given lots of freedom about how these requirements were to be met. We thought this would prevent the funders tinkering with the scope of the project, which we knew was a surefire way of making it take longer and cost more. This was the Crossrail governance model's big success. The railway that was ultimately delivered was exactly the railway that was specified at the beginning of the project. But we also knew that all this freedom from interference needed to be balanced by mechanisms that would signal if the project was going off the rails.

These would start with the leadership of Crossrail Ltd itself. An independent Chair would lead the board, on which the executive directors running the project would be outnumbered by independent non-executive directors. One of these would represent Transport for London and another the Department for Transport. Then there would be a joint Sponsor Team to act as the bridge between the company and its funders. The Sponsor Team would be deliberately small and relatively junior to avoid any tendency to meddle. But to make sure that they couldn't be misled about the status of the project, they would procure an experienced project management firm to be their Project Representative, or 'P-Rep' with wide access across the project. Finally, the contract between the funders and the company would have formal 'review points' at which the company would receive greater delegation and freedom if they could prove that they had built up the capability to manage the next phase of the project, and 'intervention thresholds' at which the funders would have the right to take direct control of the project if costs grew or the end-date was going to be missed.

Back in 2009, this had all looked sound. So how could the project have derailed so spectacularly nine years later? How could the executives in Crossrail Ltd have become so deluded about the real status of the project? And why didn't the checks and balances check and balance?

*

The Elizabeth Line is a hell of a piece of infrastructure. It is 100km long and has 41 stations, 10 of them new. It has singlehand-edly added ten percent to London's rail capacity and brought one and a half million more people to within 45 minutes of the centre of London. It links the four big commercial engines of the capital, Heathrow, the West End, the City and Canary Wharf, and on a busy day it carries nearly three-quarters of a million passengers.

Don't let a railway engineer hear you describe it like this, but in simple terms, you can think of building a railway in three phases. The first is the civil engineering, which in the case of Crossrail included boring 42km of new tunnels under the city and digging out the space for the new underground stations. Phase two is installation of all the railway systems, from the track, electrical supplies, and overhead line equipment to the signalling and com-munications kit. Alongside these you have to procure the trains themselves. The third and final phase is the integration of all those signalling and control systems with the trains, and the extensive testing and trialling of the whole railway. This starts with basic testing of whether the train will run on the track and ends with live testing of the whole service using volunteer passengers, including ticketing, access control and emergency evacuation.

For Crossrail, the civil works were a marvel. The tunnelling machines had to snake between decades worth of existing under-ground railways, electricity ducts and gas pipes, and centuries' worth of foundations of historical buildings. At one point, tun-nellers worked less than an arm's length from working tube lines. The project was rightly proud of their civil engineering triumph. The reputation of Crossrail grew as television programmes were made about it and contractors promoted their association with it. The project launched a website to broadcast its 'Learning Legacy', a 'collation and dissemination of good practice, innovation and lessons learned from the Crossrail programme aimed at raising the bar in industry and showcasing UK PLC'.[3]

On the Learning Legacy website, the Crossrail project is described as a 'huge civil engineering project with a railway run-ning through it', and it was this mindset that led to the problems that began to emerge in the second phase. Contracts were let for each of the railway systems using a tried and tested commercial approach in which the client and the contractor agree on a target-cost and share the gain of coming in cheaper and the pain of over-spend. But the problem was that the railway systems were all being designed, built and installed on the same railway at the same time. As the inevitable congestion and interfaces led to delays and extra costs, the contractors could all point the finger at one another and at Crossrail Ltd. A serious example occurred in 2017 when a large explosion at a new sub-station at Pudding Mill Lane caused major delays to testing. Most issues were less dramatic, but they all added up. Untangling the impact on everybody's costs became so complex and contentious that gradually the target-cost approach fell by the wayside and most suppliers ended up with contracts which reim-bursed their costs, with profit. Completion bonuses were intended to provide an incentive to hit the required dates, but bonuses are only an incentive if the contractor thinks the plan is realistic. And reimbursable contracts pay more if the work takes longer and uses more resource. Costs increased and the contractors' forecast com-pletion dates drifted out.

The company's approach to forecasting the ultimate cost proved disastrous. The original estimates for the project included about £2 billion of contingency. The contingency in a project is there because experience says that some of the things that might go wrong will go wrong, even if you don't know which. The trick is to make a good guess about where and when the risks are likely to materialise. In some projects the risk is mostly up front, so once the design is complete and the contracts are let, a lot of the contingency can be retired. But for the Crossrail project, a huge amount of risk was at the back end of the project. Integrating all those complex railway systems into a working railway and then testing that it all works end to end was always going to be highly risky. It was beyond optimistic to think that everything would work as expected when you put it all together. But by the time these problems began to materialise, the cost contingency had already been spent. The pres-sure on costs became acute enough early in 2018 that Transport for London and the Department negotiated an extra £500 million to take the project through to completion later that year.

A project is planned with schedule contingency, known as 'float', for exactly the same reason as for cost. But over the years in the Crossrail project, the erosion of float was masked by continuous replanning. As delays were encountered the plan was repeatedly re-baselined, but without changing the end-date. This meant that the later activities got squeezed into a tighter and tighter window. The only way to fit it in was to plan to test the signalling systems in parallel with finishing construction. This looked good on paper but actually drove inefficiency, rework and cost. Continual re-baselining gave the illusion of being on schedule, but the project was just piling up more work into the remaining available time. A realistic plan would have shown that the float was actually negative. There was not time to complete everything that had to be done, even if absolutely nothing had gone wrong. In a healthy project, the contractor's schedule is tighter than the one that the overall project is holding, which is tighter in turn than the one that the funders are banking on. In Crossrail, the inverse became the case. When contractors presented their plans for the remaining work, they were rejected because they wouldn't fit. By the time the project hit the buffers, very little of the Crossrail plan was supported by the firms who had to deliver it. Substantial delay was inevitable.

The scale of the problem during integration and testing was also disguised by the poverty of the project's management information. During construction, with a clear plan and a good cost estimate, it is not so hard to know whether you are building as quickly and spending as slowly as you planned. If your 'Schedule Performance Indicator' and your 'Cost Performance Indicator' are high, then all is well. But low numbers tell you that you're in trouble. But this doesn't work for integrating and testing something as complicated as a new railway. You can count the number of tests, but some are really easy to pass, and some are really hard. Failed tests often mean that computer coding has to be rewritten, which can mean starting the testing again from scratch. Tony Meggs, the new Chair of Crossrail Ltd after 2018, told me that it took a year to unearth the management information they really needed to understand progress.

These modes of self-deception explain why, until the wheels came off in August 2018, the project's forecast for the opening date didn't trigger intervention by the funders. And by then, there was little the funders could do except replace the management and the board and demand a whole new plan that would be deliverable this time.

*

Misuse of contingency, continual re-baselining, inappropriate planning of parallel activities, poor management information... These technical project management failings all contributed to what happened in August 2018. But how did Crossrail managers allowed themselves to be so deluded about how deeply in trouble they were?

For years, the leadership of Crossrail had been held up as the cream of British project management. The Chief Executive, Andrew Wolstenholme, had built the Heathrow Express rail link and Terminal 5 for BAA plc, both successful private sector projects. The two Programme Directors since 2009 had both had extensive rail experience. The second of them, Simon Wright, who took over from Wolstenholme as Chief Executive in April 2018, had also played a leading role in the 2012 Olympics projects. And the well-advertised success of the Crossrail civil engineering had bolstered their A-Team reputation. Tony Meggs told me that, until 2018, 'Crossrail was regarded as the golden project, the most successful complex infrastructure project in Europe.' Over the years, hubris infected the whole leadership team. Convinced of its capability, scathing about the other rail delivery organisations, and contemptuous of contrary perspectives, they came to believe their own propaganda. The issue, according to Meggs, is that 'the stronger your world perspective, the less impact contrary evidence makes'.

During the civil phase of the project, the Crossrail leaders, many of whom were experienced civil engineers, actively intervened with the contractors to solve problems as they emerged and to keep the project on track. They had repeatedly proved the doubters wrong. Later, this strength became a weakness. Faced with difficulties, they saw their job as being to put things right, not to accept defeat. They knew, by the time of the Pudding Mill Lane explosion, that their schedule was under pressure. But they convinced themselves that what had worked in the civil engineering phase would work during the railway systems phase, and that it was this very pressure that was going to drive the progress which would deliver success. Mark Wild told me that the project thought that dogmatically insisting on maintaining the end date 'would put air in the tyres, make everybody focus. Of course, what it did was increase the degree of fear as an increasingly unachievable end date approached'. I have seen this rationalisation for holding on to an impossible schedule in many government projects. If you entertain a belief that the end-date is gone, and replan with a realistic amount of float, then the pressure will come off and before you know it all the new float will be eaten up in underperformance and you are bound to have to slip again. With this mindset, it is never the right time to acknowledge that the plan is infeasible, in private or in public. For Crossrail, this might have been the right call if the likely slippage had been only a matter of a few months. But it wasn't. The painful lesson Crossrail teaches is that if you persist for too long with a schedule that nobody believes in, then one day the project goes over a cliff, and you find yourself with no plan at all.

Over-confidence born of early success, deafness to sceptical challenge, and the lack of good management information left the next generation of leaders with a project in deep trouble, and no plan.

All of this gives us a partial account for the disaster of Crossrail's 2018 announcement. But Crossrail management's delusion doesn't explain why all the defences we designed into the project's governance back in 2008 didn't prevent it happening. That explanation starts with the board of Crossrail Ltd, and in particular with the Chair, Terry Morgan. Morgan was a leading light in the civil engineering and transport project world. He had been a Fellow of the Royal Academy of Engineering for two decades, a CBE for six years and was made Sir Terry for services to infrastructure in the Queen's 2016 Birthday Honours. Less than a month before the disastrous Crossrail announcement, Transport Secretary Chris Grayling announced Morgan's appointment as Chair of the delivery company for the next huge rail project, HS2: 'His wealth of experience and expertise, demonstrated in numerous leading roles including overseeing the ambitious Crossrail project, as well as his respected reputation and enthusiasm, will be invaluable.'[4] In Crossrail, Morgan should have used his experience and expertise to challenge as well as support the company's management. In fact, he became one the biggest impediments to acknowledging reality. A senior official from the sponsor organisation told me about a conversation with Morgan in 2017.

> *I was questioning whether the project was really going to come in on time and he said, 'don't anybody dare come into my office and tell me this project's going to be late.' And guess what? No one did. The very last person in the whole of the Crossrail governance structure to accept that this thing wasn't going to be delivered on time was Terry.*

The length of Morgan's service with Crossrail may have contributed to his loss of independence. David Hughes, who led the sponsor organisation, told me that there had been consideration of board changes in 2016, 'but it was like "why would you change? There's only two years to go, it's on time and on budget, why change it?" With hindsight, that's exactly why we should have changed it'.

Morgan was supported on the board by non-executives with backgrounds in corporate governance, law, finance, economics, and urban regeneration as well as a couple with railway and engineering experience. There was more than enough nous around the board table to work out what was going wrong in the project, even in the absence of good management information. So why didn't they confront reality? The first explanation is that there was a power imbalance between the executive members, supported by the Chair, and the independent non-executives. Non-executives felt subservient to the executives, the inverse of what was required. Over time, the non-executive board ducked its responsibility to scrutinise performance and challenge the executive team. They didn't spend very much time out on the construction sites and had little engagement with suppliers. As some directors, including Wild, did come to suspect the real status, they were not able to find their voices. Everyone feared being the person who broke the golden spell. As someone in the project described it to me, 'No-one wanted to be the one who farted in church'. With limited time, lacking good data, and in the face a forceful and authoritative orthodoxy, nobody had the courage to back their own judgement. And it is not easy to prove that something is impossible.

The board didn't look as though it wanted to hear, so the board wasn't told. Those who should have presented them with a realistic picture found ways to provide updates which were factually correct but hedged to disguise the full implications. The tendency to obfuscate is so endemic in government projects that it has acquired its own label – 'strategic misrepresentation'. Older civil servants call it the 'Rhodesia solution' after a 1970s scandal in which ministers were told about British companies breaking sanctions against Rhodesia in such a way as to avoid ministers having to acknowledge the violations and act. The Rhodesia solution is damaging in government, and it can be calamitous in a project.

The Project Representative was intended as a deliberate foil to obfuscation and delusion: a small team of experienced professionals whose sole job was to present a realistic independent picture of the project's status. During the civil engineering phase of the programme they had, as was their job, raised risks and issues, many of which the project had grappled with successfully. So in the company, the P-Rep got a reputation for crying wolf. Now, when there really was a wolf, their reports were greeted with eye-rolling at the Crossrail Ltd board and were essentially ignored. In the Sponsor Team, their warnings were overwhelmed by the louder and apparently more authoritative reassurances of the company.

Through 2018, the P-Rep's reports became ever shriller, but as their warnings were filtered through the layers – the Crossrail board, the Sponsor board, the Transport for London Board and the Transport Commissioner's weekly briefing to the London Mayor, the message was lost. In March, the P-Rep wrote that,

> *The schedule is ambitious, contains virtually no float, and relies upon right-first-time delivery at productivity rates that have not been sustained in the past. There is therefore a high risk that the start dates for ... operations will not be achieved.*

It took nearly a month for the message to reach the Mayor. But by then it read,

> *Further improvement is still required to meet the milestones that deliver the Elizabeth line on December 9th 2018.*[5]

This is the Rhodesia solution in action. Given the volume of paper crossing Sadiq Khan's desk, it is little wonder that he didn't realise that one of the biggest embarrassments of his tenure was only months away.

There was one further defence against delusion that the Crossrail project managed to evade: scrutiny from the Infrastructure and Projects Authority in the Cabinet Office. For years, Crossrail Ltd was shielded from IPA reviews because it was seen as a Transport for London project rather the responsibility of central government. But eventually a review was carried out in 2015, and another in 2017. By that time, the cracks should certainly have been evident. But the reviewers expressed confidence that the railway would be completed on time and on budget. According to Tony Meggs, the IPA's Chief Executive at the time, 'The report said the right things, but it didn't say them with any urgency, and it gave the project an Amber/Green rating. I am convinced that is because the reviewers regarded this as a golden project.' Even the government's top assurers were seduced by the aura surrounding Crossrail.

*

What happened to Crossrail was a tragedy. In some of the projects I will describe in this book, the seeds of failure were sown into them right from the start. But this is far less true of Crossrail. It was, through much of its life, a sound and healthy project. The strategic case for the railway was clear and consistent throughout and its scope remained remarkably stable. The railway, now that it is finished, is fulfilling its potential and will be a core component of the capital's transport infrastructure throughout the twenty-first century.

Had the reality of the railway systems and integration challenge been acknowledged earlier, when the signs were all there to be read, the politics of a delay, although painful, could have been navigated. Opinions vary, but according to Mark Wild, the CEO who rescued the project, 'We ended up being four years and four billion out. I would have said you could have done it for a lot less than that. Perhaps as much as half of the overrun was preventable with earlier action.'

The governance put in place at the beginning should have been sufficient. If the executives had had more introspection and been actively seeking alternative views. If the Chair, as well as being a champion for the project externally, had retained perspective internally. If the non-executives had been more curious, avoided groupthink, and been less cowed by the reputation of the management. And if the internal reporters and external scrutineers had been braver, and more skilled at speaking truth to power.

These are very human failings. Hubris, myopia, self-protection and fear.

I don't think any of the players in the Crossrail drama would act in the same way now. None of them has gained anything except painful learning from bitter experience. Careers ended prematurely and reputations were tarnished. But the underlying incentives which drove Crossrail off the rails haven't changed. And neither has human nature.

But unfortunately, the next projects are going to be led by humans too. So unless we can tilt the incentive structures, to increase the pressure to do the right thing and reduce the perceived penalty for speaking out, then we will never eliminate the possibility of the failings of Crossrail being repeated. We will have to do something different.

The next chapter is about a project that couldn't even achieve the part that Crossrail got right – a clear, stable, and resilient scope. Its origins go back not just to before Crossrail, but to 1834, three decades before London's very first underground train entered service.

4

VACILLATION AND PARALYSIS: THE PALACE OF WESTMINSTER

Lord Melbourne, Queen Victoria's Whig Prime Minister, called the decision to burn cartloads of wooden tally sticks in the furnaces under the House of Lords 'one of the greatest instances of stupidity upon record'.[1] Fire smouldered in the furnace chimney for hours before it spread, eventually consuming most of the Palace of Westminster. Construction of a new Parliament building began in 1840. The design for Charles Barry's gothic masterpiece was chosen in a blind competition from among nearly a hundred others. He said it would take six years to build and cost an exorbitant three quarters of a million pounds. But public sector project failures are nothing new, and it was twelve years before members of the Commons sat in their new chamber, and another eighteen before the whole project was completed.

Nearly two centuries later, report after report has warned that history could repeat itself. Every couple of months on average, an incident that could lead to fire in the Palace is prevented by fire-watchers who are required to patrol the building at all hours. The subterranean ducts and shafts, designed by Barry as an innovative heating and ventilation system have, over the decades, been crammed higgledy-piggledy with pipes and cables for services never dreamed off in the 1830s – power, water, data and communications, heating, air conditioning and fire detection. In the event of a fire, the remaining shafts would chimney smoke through the building in no time. And it is not just the fire risk that is a problem. Most of the building's services have been obsolete for years and the drawings are poor to non-existent. Pollution has eaten away at the stonework and stories of falling masonry are common. The roofs leak, allowing damp to penetrate many parts of the Palace. Leaking pipes periodically cause floods. There is asbestos everywhere.

If nothing is done, then one day something catastrophic is going to happen. Nobody knows precisely what or when it will occur, but when it does it might mean the Mother of Parliaments having to find another home.

This diagnosis has hardly changed since the turn of the century, when further patching of the mechanical, electrical, water, drainage and sanitation systems was declared to be uneconomic. In 2012 a study group appointed by the Management Boards of both Houses famously declared that 'if the Palace were not a listed building of the highest heritage value, its owners would probably be advised to demolish and rebuild'.[2] Four years later, a committee of both Houses told their members that the Palace was facing 'an impending crisis which we cannot responsibly ignore... Unless an intensive programme of major remedial work is undertaken soon, it is likely that the building will become uninhabitable'.[3] A further report warned three years later that

> the building is deteriorating faster than it can be repaired... There is therefore an urgent and pressing need to plan and deliver a major project that allows for a full and comprehensive restoration and renewal of the Palace of Westminster.[4]

All that has changed over the years is that the condition of the Palace has deteriorated, the obsolete systems are even more antiquated, and the risks are higher.

But it is one thing to diagnose the illness and quite another to agree on a cure. The meandering saga of indecision about how to address the state of the Palace would fill a tedious book on its own, but it can be summarised like this. In 2009, a group of officials from both Houses proposed a plan to replace the systems in the basements and ducts over a 10-year period without disrupting the work of Parliament. But the Management Boards of the two Houses decided it was too risky and, in any case, didn't deal with the whole problem. Instead, they decided on a rolling programme of repairs to buy time to decide what to do for the long term. They appointed a study group, which reported in 2012. There were really only three options, the group reported: either vacate the Palace completely as the restoration work was undertaken, vacate each House in turn, or try and continue the day-to-day workings of both Houses while work went on around them. The study group was in no doubt which option was the best. Working around both Houses was a non-starter, and dividing the Palace into a building site at one end and a functioning Parliament at the other would bring 'near insurmountable security risks'.[5] Parliament's response was to commission a new independent appraisal of options, which was completed in 2014, but not published until after the 2015 election. The conclusion was the same. Vacating the Palace was the only feasible option. A joint committee of both Houses was appointed to consider the conclusions, but the turmoil following the Brexit referendum meant that it took until the end of 2016 for it to endorse the findings. Parliament would indeed, they concluded, have to move out of the Palace. Their proposal was that the House of Commons would move up Whitehall to a government building opposite the Cenotaph called Richmond House. The Lords would move into the brutalist Queen Elizabeth II Conference Centre, opposite Westminster Abbey. Making these two venues fit to house the two chambers would be a major programme of work in itself, not to mention the need to find offices for the thousands of people that it takes to support the operations of Parliament.

Meanwhile, tackling the crumbling stonework of Big Ben and the Elizabeth Tower, at the northern end of the Palace, could be put off no longer, and the clock itself was reported to have as little as two or three years of bongs left in it. In 2017, the chimes went silent, and the tower disappeared under scaffolding for four years in a job that was estimated at £29 million but eventually cost £80 million. Disappointed tourists, with nothing to photograph, would have been forgiven for concluding that the long-awaited refurbishment of the Palace was underway. But in fact, nothing had yet been decided.

After the 2017 election in which Theresa May lost her Conservative majority, the Prime Minister appointed her erstwhile leadership rival Andrea Leadsom to be Leader of the House of Commons. The business of the chamber was dominated by Brexit, but Leadsom also inherited the headache of the condition of the building.

> *When I was first leader, we had some absolutely shocking stone masonry falls. One over Black Rod's entrance, where all the school children go in, and another when a gargoyle fell off onto the windscreen of my deputy leader's car. I went for a basement tour with a couple of the project team only to find that a sewage pipe had burst and so there was neat sewage just spraying all over the place.*

She was also briefed on Parliament's contingency plan for adoption in the event of a now all-too-likely problem with the Palace.

> *The contingency was to use the QE2 centre, and it was so Heath Robinson that it was clearly utterly inadequate. That was, for me, the final nail in the coffin and I thought, right, we need to take this seriously.*

So amidst the chaos of Parliament's Brexit brawling, Leadsom also needed MPs to endorse the joint committee's recommendation to fully vacate the Palace for the duration of the restoration project. In that debate, there were impassioned pleas for action from those who had toured the Palace basements or served on the numerous committees and boards that had examined the options over the years. But there were also plenty of sceptics. A Dorset MP with a professional background in public relations accused Leadsom of catastrophising.

> *We hear the Armageddon scenario that we are going to be washed away in slurry, burnt to death or electrocuted, and yet we have thousands of visitors from the public in this place every day. I see no signs to say, 'Welcome to the death trap'.*[6]

Edward Leigh, future Father of the House, had sought his own second opinion.

> *I commissioned an architect, pro bono, who proved con-*
> *clusively that [remaining in the palace] would be perfectly*
> *possible... Are we really being told that in this day and age*
> *we cannot divert sewerage and electrical wiring? They do*
> *it all the time in the private sector.*

And arch-traditionalist Jacob Rees-Mogg asked, 'Are we really so precious that there must never even be the slightest sound of a hammer bashing a nail into a piece of wood?'. But the two most common protests were the politically pragmatic argument that the cost couldn't be justified to constituents, and the romantically historic case that continuity of governing the country on the site must never be broken. 'When the chips were down in 1941, Clement Attlee and Winston Churchill decided that this Chamber would not move from this building.'

Despite the tacit support of the Prime Minister and Chief Whip, the free vote on the joint committee's recommendations was won by only 16 votes. But once the proposal was supported in the House of Lords, Parliament had now apparently finally made up its mind. It would move out.

Work began on a bill to allow the project to proceed. In October 2018, the Draft Parliamentary Buildings (Restoration and Renewal) Bill was published, and a new joint committee was appointed to conduct pre-legislative scrutiny. But the only subject on Parliament's mind was Brexit. Prime Minister May was losing vote after vote on the Withdrawal Agreement, and hundreds of thousands of pro-EU protesters marched in Parliament Square demanding a re-run of the referendum. Who knows how long it might have taken for the Bill to be passed had not Parliament's meandering considerations received an injection of energy in mid-April 2019 when Notre Dame in Paris burnt down. Within weeks, the Bill was introduced in the House of Commons and, despite the turmoil of new Prime Minister Boris Johnson's attempt to prorogue Parliament, and his expulsion of rebel MPs from the Conservative party, in September the Bill received Royal Assent.

The Act set out how the project, now routinely called Restoration and Renewal, R&R, would be governed. In some ways, the drafters had had to wrestle with the same conundrums that had faced funders in the Crossrail Project. First, the interests of the two Houses, like those of the Mayor of London and the Transport Secretary, might not always align, and second, a way had to be found to distance delivery of the work from too much political interference. Their answer was similar too. A delivery authority would be set up to lead the project at arm's length from the normal business of Parliament. Its first Chief Executive, David Goldstone, was a veteran of major Whitehall delivery, having overseen finance on the Olympic projects and been the Chief Operating Officer of the Ministry of Defence. Goldstone had seen arm's length delivery bodies succeed spectacularly – and fail catastrophically. The appointment was widely regarded as a coup for the project. An independent board would be chaired by Mike Brown, Commissioner of Transport for London, who had learnt lessons from the Crossrail debacle about how to manage the interface between sponsors and deliverers. Brown's new non-executive directors had experience in all the right disciplines.

Established at the same time was a Sponsor Body. Perhaps learning from Crossrail, where the joint Sponsor Team lacked the weight to stand up to Crossrail Ltd, the R&R Sponsor Body had its own hefty board, with experts in construction, regeneration, heritage, and finance as well as seven members from across the two Houses. Parliament would be the ultimate funder and customer for the work but would no longer be running the programme. The final governance layer was an Estates Commission made up of two Lords and two Commons members. Their job was to scrutinise the Sponsor Body's spending estimates and to recommend approval to the House of Commons, who ultimately had to agree the budget.

After a decade of consideration, everything now seemed to be in place for the project to proceed. Both Houses had voted to vacate the Palace, and both had decided where they would go. The structures for delivery of the project were set up and beginning to work. It was all systems go. When I met with David Goldstone in the weeks after he stood down from the Delivery Authority in 2024, he told me,

> *Trusting the decision that had been made, we bashed on*
> *and started developing a business case to get the formal*

*approval for a scope that was properly costed with sched-
ule and risk. We were planning to take that to the Houses
for approval in early 2023. But we never got to the actual
decision.*

The narrowness of the Commons 2018 vote should have been a
warning of what was to come.

The first act of the new Sponsor Body was to undertake, through
the Delivery Authority, a strategic review of how the project would
be done, and to estimate how much it would cost and how long it
would take. Mindful perhaps of the closeness of the 2018 vote, the
Speaker of the House of Commons, Lindsay Hoyle, also asked the
Sponsor Body to assess the possibility of keeping the Commons in
the Palace during the work. The Sponsor Body provided an initial
assessment, confirming the impracticality of continued presence,
but declined to do more on the grounds that they had neither the
time nor the funds. After the strategic review was published, the
Sponsor Body revealed the cost estimates to the Commissions of
the two Houses of Parliament in January 2022. Providing new
homes for the Houses, moving out, refurbishing, and moving
back, would cost an eye-watering £7 billion to 13 billion and take
between 19 and 28 years. The Palace would be uninhabitable for
between 12 and 20 of those years.[7]

The Delivery Authority had done just as it was asked by the
Sponsor Body – and the Sponsor Body had asked the Delivery
Authority for exactly what Parliament had laid down. But nobody
was happy. According to Goldstone,

*There were two big problems. There was just this perva-
sive view that we can't possibly go out to the public and
say we're going to spend north of £10 billion on MP's
offices in central London when the country was in the economic situation it was in. And second, quite a strong feeling that it was not tenable for the House of Commons in
particular to not operate in its traditional chamber for the
length of time it was going to need. These came together
in a feeling that there must be a different way that's lower
impact in terms of time and cost and that only does what
has to be done.*

Goldstone is adamant that the Delivery Authority's plans were not gold-plated. 'I'm proud of the fact that, hand on heart, nobody ever said they didn't trust the work we did. They really just didn't like the outcome.' Not liking the answer, Parliament decided that the problem must be the governance structure that it had itself put in place. Different governance would surely give a better answer. Building a substantial and capable Sponsor Body, in response to the Crossrail experience, had backfired. The two Commissions (each consisting of parliamentarians and lay-members, and chaired by the Speaker) proposed a new approach which was supported by the two Houses. The Sponsor Body would be abolished, and its functions and staff brought back in-house to report to the Clerks of the two Houses. The two Commissions would act as a Client Board to decide on strategy and make recommendations to the Houses. And to try to make sure that the recommendations would stick this time, there would be a new advisory Programme Board made up of members from both Houses, Palace officials and independent members with project expertise.

By the end of the year, the new structure was in place, but the decision making – on what to do and how to do it – was back to square one. Goldstone told me.

> I very vividly remember the meeting when it became clear that the decision they were going to make would be to stop all work on the business case. We went back quite quickly and said, in effect, that 'you've decided you don't want all the things you had previously decided you did want, but you don't know what you do want'. The only way we could see forward was to take them back to the wide range of options for what the scope of restoration could involve – and how it could be delivered.

After costing the single option on which both Houses had agreed, the new strategy was to go back to the beginning and present as wide a range of options as could reasonably be contemplated. The Delivery Authority agreed to work on 6 levels of ambition for the renovation, and 6 options for how to deliver it, meaning 36 options in total.

By 2023, the smorgasbord of options was ready to present to the Programme Board. The Board opted for the fifth of six scope options, which was essentially the same scheme that the Delivery Authority had presented in January 2022. They didn't go for the cheaper options that wouldn't have met building regulations, or the more ambitious plan which would have provided resilience against climate change and reintroduced historical details that had been lost to the weathering of time. As for the delivery options, the Programme Board was unable to decide whether to support fully leaving the Palace during the work, or whether to try to keep the Commons inside the Palace while the work was done around it. The Client Board accepted the Programme Board's recommendation but inserted another option at the insistence of the House of Commons Commission. This option had a label, 'Enhanced Maintenance and Improvement', but as yet little definition. The idea seemed to be to modernise the Palace piecemeal without disturbing the business of Parliament. These were, in other words, the same three options first put forward in 2012: Move out completely while the work is done, partially move out but keep one chamber working throughout, or try to do the work without leaving. The first seems politically impossible, the third seems physically impossible, and the second looks like the worst of all worlds.

Having left the Delivery Authority after five frustrating years, David Goldstone's nervousness is whether the organisation can be held together for much longer.

> We set up a really good delivery machine, with people who really wanted to do it and who had the right mix of skills and capabilities. We were good to go. We got pushed right back in 2022, and then we got good to go again. If they spend years more making the decision, they might look around and find there's no one there to deliver it.

*

In some ways, the R&R project is a special case. Parliament is particularly unsuited to sponsoring a very large project. With no equivalent of a Secretary of State, nobody is really in charge. But governments too sometimes find it impossible to decide either to proceed with, or to abandon, a project. For two decades, successive governments have repeatedly tried and failed to get a project to tunnel past Stonehenge up and running. They have also failed to approve a project to decongest the road network of eastern England by tunnelling under the lower Thames. Both have been announced many times, but neither has been approved. Projects for commercial scale Carbon Capture and Storage have been launched three times since 2007. Funding was allocated to the task again in Labour's post-election budget in 2024, but there is no certainty that this attempt will fly either. The search for a location for a geological disposal facility for the country's nuclear waste began in the 1970s. Fifty years and many attempts later, there is still no agreed site. Why do governments find projects so hard to get off the ground?

Sometimes it is as simple as there being no economically or politically acceptable project available. Every project can be thought of as a delivery triangle. One side is the scope – what is to be done – and the others are how long it will take and what it will cost. And in every case, there is another triangle, rarely openly acknowledged, which defines what size and shape of project will be able to garner enough support to be authorised. If your delivery triangle fits comfortably within the acceptability triangle, then the project might be worth developing. But if the scope doesn't work politically, or if you can't afford it, or if it will take too long, then you have a problem. This is exactly where the R&R project finds itself. 'Listen', a member of the Programme Board told his colleagues, 'you can pontificate as much as you like, but the reality is nobody is going to be voting for a multi-billion-pound project on themselves at a time when cuts are being made in other sectors'.[8] None of the delivery triangles that Parliament is once again reconsidering fits in the acceptability triangle. They either don't deliver the required scope, cost too much, or take too long. If you can't increase the size of the acceptability triangle, or reshape the delivery triangle to fit within it, you are really better off not starting. And the earlier you reach this conclusion the better. The problem is that actually deciding not to do a project is often as politically problematic as deciding to do it. Parliament is unlikely to announce that it has decided to live with the dangerous condition of the Palace. They have proved themselves capable of believing strongly that 'something must be done', while repeatedly concluding that 'this isn't it!'. Governments have the same incentive to vacillate. It is particularly strong with very large and lengthy projects. The pain of an unpopular decision comes right now. The cost and disruption are both explicit and proximate. But the benefits won't be felt for a decade or more and the risks of delay tend to be nebulous and difficult to quantify.

The path of least resistance is to push off the decision to your successors. And you can do that by repeatedly chasing a mirage that will deliver all your policy objectives, but also fit within the acceptability triangle. This is why R&R, the Lower Thames Crossing project, and the Geological Disposal Facility project, are stuck in an apparently endless loop of optioneering and re-evaluation while the risk of a disaster in the Palace grows year by year, traffic congestion inhibits growth in eastern England, and nuclear sites build expensive stores to contain waste until the ultimate disposal solution is finally approved.

But sometimes governments take an even worse course than endless re-evaluation. Sometimes ministers, officials, and deliverers, faced with a delivery triangle which doesn't fit, conspire to force the project into the acceptability triangle with a hammer. Low-balling the early estimates of cost and schedule may help to get the project approved, but they bake failure into it right from the start. Ironically, the fact that this hasn't happened on the R&R project is a credit to the professionalism of the Delivery Authority. It has resisted the temptation to under-estimate the scale of the challenge.

*

David Goldstone told me that he is still confident that the project would, one day, get the go-ahead.

> We've now got a client construct that's more than capable of making decisions. And they know they can't do nothing. The risk with protracted delay is the increasing likelihood of a serious incident, or that Parliament could start running out of road of being safe. They ... could start

having to take areas out of use because they can't maintain them to a safe level.

Andrea Leadsom is less confident.

I think the nature of our democracy is going to make it extremely difficult to ever resurrect the option of moving out. No government is going to want to be seen to sanction that expense. So in truth I suspect there will be some catastrophic failure that kicks us out. Realistically, the best outcome would be to have a proper contingency.

Another ex-MP told me, 'You know, if you test it to destruction – then it will destruct!'.

So the nature of our democracy might just cost us the home of our democracy. I wonder what Lord Melbourne would think of that.

5

BLIND AMBITION: UNIVERSAL CREDIT

While indecision was paralysing the Restoration and Renewal project in the Palace of Westminster, the Universal Credit project had precisely the opposite problem. It hared off at a hundred miles an hour without the first idea how it was going to reach its destination.

By 2010, after decades of evolution, the UK's welfare benefits were a rat's nest of policies and systems that even welfare professionals found it hard to navigate. For some of those eligible for benefits, understanding their entitlements was complicated to the point of impossibility. The hotchpotch wasn't only a poor way of getting support to those who needed it, but it was expensive to administer and open to fraud. But beneath the problem of effectiveness, there was a deeper concern. Politicians on left and right, as well as many policy officials in the Department for Work and Pensions, believed that the welfare regime was actually trapping men and women, families and even whole communities in deprivation and dependency, sustaining and exacerbating the very symptoms that the benefits system was intended to alleviate. Whether you were suffering from a disability, or out of work for other reasons, benefits were an active disincentive to working. Why would you forego the predictable security of a benefits cheque for the risky business of taking a job which might not last, or which you might not be able to manage? This concern led successive governments to imagine a welfare system which rewarded work. If you retained some of your benefits when you began to earn and regained them without fuss if your job didn't work out, the barrier to work would be much lower. As claimants earned more, their benefits would gradually and smoothly taper off until, ultimately, fewer people would be without a wage and fewer households would be without work. If only we could start again with a simpler, more rational welfare system, then benefits recipients would be better off, make a greater contribution to the economy, and pay more tax. And the welfare bill, heading towards £200 billion by 2010, would come down. There was genuine political passion behind this idea in the run up to the 2010 election.

The clearest enunciation of the policy came not from either front bench in Parliament, but from Tory backbencher Iain Duncan Smith. IDS, as he was universally known, had led the Conservative Party between 2001 and 2003. But, unable to retain the confidence of his party in the wake of poor local election results and an expenses scandal, he spent the rest of the decade on the back benches, pouring his energy into a think-tank, the Centre for Social Justice. IDS's scheme would replace a total of 51 existing benefits with a single universal, but dynamic, payment. The fundamental idea was that as a welfare recipient earns an extra pound, they would retain 45p of their benefit cheque. Work would always pay, and the welfare trap would become instead a virtuous cycle encouraging people out of poverty and out of dependency.[1]

Meanwhile, the Labour government had co-opted David Freud, an investment banker with an interest in the benefits system, to advise a series of Work and Pensions Secretaries on how to get more claimants into work. Shadow Chancellor George Osborne, ever on the lookout for political advantage, spotted an opportunity to undermine Labour's traditional lead on welfare. He poached Freud from Labour in 2009 by convincing David Cameron to nominate him for the House of Lords. Freud became a shadow minister under the shadow Work and Pensions Secretary, Theresa May. Cameron hadn't anticipated making IDS, with his evangelical views on welfare, Work and Pensions Secretary, but coalition with the Liberal Democrats forced him to shuffle his pack, which resulted in Theresa May landing in the Home Office and IDS taking on DWP, with Freud as his Minister of State for Welfare Reform.[2]

IDS's policy ideas landed on fertile ground in the Department and a coalition of believers formed around him and Freud. In no time a new project, Universal Credit, was born. The plan was to introduce a single benefit, of the kind envisioned by the Centre for Social Justice, to replace DWP's big three means-tested benefits, Job Seekers Allowance, Income Support, Employment and Support Allowance, as well as Child Tax Credits and Working Tax Credits, administered by HMRC, and Housing Benefit, which was paid by Local Authorities. Non-means tested benefits, like Child Support, were excluded because middle-class recipients, many of them Tory voters, would inevitably lose out. The Universal Credit system would not only simplify the landscape, but it would also be dynamic, adjusting the payments benefit to account for fluctuations in earnings.

Outside DWP, warning bells began to ring immediately about the scale of the IT challenge. The Coalition government was, after all, in the processes of euthanising a number of failed Labour IT projects, from the Identity Cards Scheme to the electronic transformation of border controls. How, for example, would the new DWP systems know how much someone earned quickly enough to calculate the amount of benefit they would get? Would it be from their employer, their bank, or HMRC's income tax system? David Cameron's troubleshooter, Jeremy Heywood, paid particular attention to the project through a series of meetings in the Cabinet Office and Number 10, several of them including Cameron and Osborne as well as the DWP ministers and senior officials. Accounts of what happened behind these closed doors vary. IDS and Freud insist that they put no pressure on departmental officials to understate the challenge. Others say that the project envisioned at that point was simpler than the one which subsequently developed. Whatever the truth, the DWP Permanent Secretary Leigh Lewis signed off a submission which described the IT development as being of only moderate scale, and reassured Heywood that the Department and its IT suppliers were confident of delivering it on time.[3]

With that understanding, the new ministerial team laid out their plans in a consultation paper within weeks of the election.

The paper insisted that the implementation would not require a major IT programme but would be delivered by 'building on existing technologies'.[4] By November, a White Paper launched the process of developing the required primary and secondary legislation. The Prime Minister told the *Financial Times* that Universal Credit was 'one of the boldest and most radical reforms since Beveridge'.[5] In fact, this was the point at which IDS doomed the project by announcing a fixed timetable for delivery. The regulations, he said, would be finalised by 2012 and Universal Credit would be available as a live service in October 2013. Transferring existing claimants would be complete by 2017, at which point the legacy benefits would fall away. Although the White Paper described the timeline as provisional, from this point on, IDS took both the 2013 start date and the 2017 end date to be firm commitments. Nothing must prevent them being achieved. In his opening remarks in the White Paper, he trumpeted that, 'Successive governments have ignored the need for fundamental welfare reform, not because they didn't think that reform was needed but because they thought it too difficult to achieve.' But the paper had no mention of implementation risks or challenges.

The unrealistic timetable may have helped to get the project announced, but it also nurtured distrust in its stakeholders across government. From that moment forward, the project was beset by vetoers and anti-sponsors, and overwhelmed by reviewers and auditors. Treasury officials were against the project from the start. This may have been partly institutional scepticism, born of long experience, about whether the economic benefits of any big IT-enabled project would flow as promised. But they also worried about the cost of compensating the losers who would inevitably be created in the transition. They preferred a more direct way of reducing the benefits bill. Rather than embark on a potentially long and risky project, why not simply reduce benefits as part of the austerity programme and impose more conditionality on payments? Stories about blazing rows between IDS and Osborne surfaced in the national press.[6]

But it wasn't just the Treasury. Francis Maude, the new Cabinet Office Minister, was on a mission to change the way IT projects and services were delivered.[7] Before long, this would bring conflict between the Cabinet Office and the Department for Work and Pensions.

Although even the primary legislation would not be passed for another 18 months, let alone the detailed regulations, by the time the White Paper was published, the DWP's IT service providers were already working on the systems required to make Universal Credit work. These were the companies that had delivered the systems for the legacy benefits that Universal Credit would replace, most recently the Employment and Support Allowance, which had been rolled out with little fuss. But ESA had followed an IT project delivery methodology which was now regarded as being old, inflexible and slow. Universal Credit was going to be delivered by following the new vogue for IT projects – Agile development. The traditional way of developing IT systems is to spend time up-front defining in detail exactly what the system has to do. Then the computer code is written, and the system is tested every which-way to check that it does what was intended. IT project people call this a waterfall approach as though each stage were one pool in a series of cataracts – the point being that you can only go down the waterfall, you can't go back. Everything happens sequentially and complicated systems can take years to build. This isn't the place for a full description of Agile development, but the idea is that code gets written in short sharp bursts which are tested as you go along. Development is theoretically much faster, and because rework and retesting are part of the process, incorporation of tweaks and changes is much easier. Agile development wasn't completely new in 2010, but after the election it was adopted in some government projects like a new religion, complete with its own language. Individual bursts of development were 'scrums' carried out in 'sprints'. For Universal Credit, the IT providers began by working on the simplest possible case – a new single claimant with no dependents – with the idea of adding more complicated cases progressively. But DWP's suppliers had never delivered Agile projects on anything as complex as the UK welfare system. Without experience and a bedrock of capability, the theoretical benefits of the approach were hard to find in practice. Compounding the confused start to the development work was the project's collision with another new Cabinet Office initiative – 'digital by default'.

Martha Lane Fox, founder of the on-line travel company last-minute.com and the government's new 'Digital Champion', recommended to Maude that paper-based government services should become a thing of the past. She proposed that a new CEO for Digital in the Cabinet Office should be given 'absolute authority over the user experience across all government online services and the power to direct all government online spending'. The urgent subtitle of her report was 'Revolution not Evolution'.[8] Another new orthodoxy was born. It was unthinkable that Universal Credit, the new government's flagship services development, should be delivered in the old-fashioned way with paper forms filled in at Jobcentres. Universal Credit would have to be a digital service. But as with Agile development, a wholly digital solution brought problems as well as opportunities. Soon the scale of the IT challenge was becoming undeniable. The development sprints were delivering less than planned and the project was struggling to find a way to access a claimant's earnings to allow the benefit top-up to be calculated dynamically. By the end of the year, the project was signalling a six-month delay to system development. Meanwhile, concerns about security were beginning to undermine confidence that what was being built would be fit for purpose. Some were beginning to whisper that the whole development would need to be started again, this time with security built in from the beginning rather than bolted on at the end. Gradually the project began to water down its ambition for which claimants would be covered by the first release of Universal Credit, and in how many places.

But IDS would not countenance any delay. According to Freud, 'Iain had a way of asserting what he wished to be the case.'[9] Rather than face reality, the project instead decided that something – anything – must go live by April 2013, six months earlier than the planned service commencement. They called it a 'pathfinder' and promoted it as a way of reducing risk for the full launch. As confidence in the 2013 launch withered further, IDS dug in. 'I've made a very clear commitment to all my colleagues, including the Prime Minister and the Chancellor, that we are able to deliver this – so the Department needs to push hard and make all the changes required.'[10]

The gap between expectations and reality created a punishing atmosphere within the project team. In this kind of environment, even excellent people will wilt. An early casualty was the project's first leader, Terry Moran, who suffered a breakdown and took early retirement.[11] Towards the end of 2012, security worries drove Philip Langsdale, the next official to lead the project, to launch a review of the technical foundations on which the system was being built. But tragedy struck when Langsdale fell ill and died over Christmas. By now, the Cabinet Office had joined the Treasury in having serious concerns about how the Universal Credit project was being run. Maude's two weapons were the Major Projects Authority and the new Government Digital Service, which was now up and running as the government's digitisation expert in response to Martha Lane Fox's recommendations. Maude was determined to reduce government's dependence on large IT suppliers and briefly mulled plans to take the DWP's suppliers to court for their performance on Universal Credit.[12] But in reality, the causes were home grown. The Major Projects Authority told the project team that its fundamental problem was the lack of a clear definition of what the service would look like when it was complete. It needed what they described as a 'blueprint'. With IDS's agreement, Maude parachuted David Pitchford, the Major Project Authority's Chief Executive, into the project to sort it out. But in May 2013, just months before the intended go-live, Pitchford's crushing message was that, once a blueprint was agreed, a completely new digital system would be required. Rather than focussing on a tiny slice of claimants before working towards more complicated claims, it would be developed to take the full range of cases right from the beginning. It would target serving just one hundred people at a new go-live date in spring 2014 and build up slowly to 10,000 claimants by the end of that year. The Department would have to abandon all the development work undertaken by its IT providers and create a completely new team of coders inside DWP, sourced initially from the new Government Digital Service.

By now, nobody in the project really believed that a meaningful service could be rolled out from the original date. But that didn't stop IDS reconfirming the dates to the Work and Pensions Select Committee. 'Between October 2013 and 2017, all those who fall

within the ambit of Universal Credit will be on Universal Credit.'
Sitting next to him was Howard Shiplee, who had replaced David
Pitchford as the latest new official in charge of the project. Shiplee
was an experienced project manager, fresh from the 2012 Olympics
construction projects, but he had no background in either IT
projects or the Department. He backed up the Secretary of State's
assertion. 'I see no reason why this programme cannot be delivered
within the due dates that have been established and within the
budgets that have been allocated to us.'[13]

But Universal Credit was government's first major self-delivered
IT solution in more than a decade. Soon the digital team was forecasting that it would not be ready to begin roll-out until sometime in 2015. This was met by a rearguard action from within the
Department to try and save the nearly three years' worth of work
that had already been undertaken by the IT providers. Maude was
convinced that this was motivated by trying to avoid the embar-
rassment of exposing a large financial write-off in the Department's
accounts. The relationship between the Cabinet Office and the project hit an all-time low. By November, the two competing delivery
strategies – press on with the IT providers' solution despite concerns about its security, or start again with a brand-new digital
system – had become fused into a single twin-track approach. The
emerging plan was to begin roll-out at a very small scale on the IT
providers' systems. These would serve a tiny number of the simplest
claimants in just one or two Jobcentres, while in the background
the new digital solution would be built. Maude was furious. The
Government Digital Service declared that Universal Credit was no
longer an 'exemplar' project, and they would no longer support
it. Without the cachet of Cabinet Office support, the Department
struggled to recruit experienced IT developers and found itself rely-
ing on a large number of very expensive freelance contractors.

By the end of 2013, the project's roll-out plan extended into the
spring of 2019. But IDS wanted the Department to hold publicly
to the 2017 commitment. He was convinced to soften his stance to
'most' claimants being on Universal Credit by the deadline. Meanwhile, the baby-steps of roll-out continued. Through 2014, the service extended to a small number of couples without children, and it
was hoped to soon move on to parents. But this was achieved only

with many manual workarounds and a lot of Jobcentre staff effort. By the summer, the plan for 'most' claimants to be on Universal Credit by 2017 was already looking undeliverable.

The only good news available to the project was that by the end of the year a handful of claimants were finally receiving Universal Credit through the new digital system. This breakthrough provided the first glimpse of a route out of the hole the project had dug for itself. By now, Shiplee had departed due to ill-health and the project was being run by a DWP insider, Neil Couling, who remained the project's senior leader for the next 10 years. The rest of the story can be told more quickly. After the 2015 election surprised even the Conservatives by giving them a working majority, George Osborne tried to convince David Cameron to move IDS out of DWP, but the Prime Minister wanted to keep him where he was.[14] IDS eventually resigned in March 2016 in protest at cuts to disability allowance, which he portrayed as the final straw in his battle with the Treasury.

A post-election plan to expand the digital rollout for new claimants to 50 of the 600 Jobcentres by early 2017 actually took until Sept 2018, but, nonetheless, real progress was being made. It was time to begin thinking about migrating the claimants who were still on legacy benefits over to Universal Credit. It was intended to start this in July 2019 and conclude in 2022. The Covid pandemic proved to be a turning point of sorts for Universal Credit. Migration of existing claimants was paused, but Covid lockdowns led to new applicants, which had the effect of doubling the numbers on the system in the course of 2020. Many insiders think that the legacy systems simply would not have coped with this influx. Once the pandemic was over, with caution born of experience, Couling now began to migrate only those claimants whose circumstances had changed. Those whose situation was unchanged, who tended to be the most vulnerable, would receive careful treatment, even if this meant that the migration would continue for many more years.

The project was finally acknowledging the reality that welfare is intrinsically complex. People are unique, and their individual situations are complicated and difficult to navigate. Throughout the early years of the project, its complexity was systematically underestimated. Three of many examples will illustrate the point. Firstly, receiving some legacy benefits opened the door to other services like free prescriptions, free school meals, and legal aid. If all the benefits merged into one, then what would happen to these 'passported' services? Would they too become 'universal'? Secondly, it became policy to make Universal Credit payments monthly rather than weekly as a way of treating recipients as though they were employees. But weeks don't fit neatly into months and this transition proved to be a nightmare to code. Thirdly, policy required that housing allowance should be paid to the benefits claimant rather than their landlord. Everyone else pays their own bills – why should that be different just because someone is receiving support from the state? But not everyone can manage their spending to cope with monthly payments, or will ensure that money received for their housing costs will actually make it into the hands of the landlord. David Freud described building dozens of simple-sounding policies like these into Universal Credit as 'headbangingly difficult'.[15] The complexity was compounded by the need to coordinate delivery well beyond DWP and its 600 Jobcentres. There was significant change required in HMRC and all 380 Local Authorities. And the Cabinet Office owned the functional standards for digital services as well as being a powerful observer, critic, and judge sitting on the sidelines. Finally, GCHQ was the ultimate guardian of digital security.

A Cabinet minister from the time told me that he still believed that Universal Credit should have been delivered to the original timeframe. 'It was perfectly possible, but the DWP had no idea how to do it.' In fact, it should have been obvious right at the outset that the promised delivery schedule was simply impossible. The current forecast is that legacy benefits will not be turned off until 2029 – 12 years later than IDS originally promise.

*

Judged against the original schedule, failure was built into the Universal Credit project from the beginning. So why did ministers and officials lock themselves into an undeliverable plan?

The report David Freud wrote for the Labour government in 2007 forecast that a new benefits system would take eight years to introduce.[16] Eight years was also the prediction that the

Conservatives were given by PWC at around the same time. But the thought in IDS's mind, dating back to his Centre for Social Justice report, was that the whole transformation, including retiring all the legacy benefits, had to be completed within a single Parliamentary term. So, in government, his question was not 'why do we think we can launch in 2013?', but 'why do we have to wait that long?' His political strategy was, in the words of one senior official, 'One year to make policy, three years to implement, and one year to crow about it'. But there was enough knowledge and experience in the Department to know that such an outcome was, to say the very least, extremely unlikely. So why did officials go along with it?

Both Freud and IDS have denied pressuring the Department to adopt the October 2013 launch date. Indeed, Freud records several occasions in which departmental IT leaders assured him that it would be possible. It is rare in Whitehall for ministers to demand that officials implement decisions when they believe them to be a poor use of public money. There are rules to protect officials when this does happen. A recent example of this protection was the formal written instruction that Home Office Permanent Secretary Matthew Rycroft required from Home Secretary Priti Patel to develop the scheme to deport asylum seekers to Rwanda. But in most projects, the incentives on officials are subtler than this kind of formal ministerial direction. Put yourself in the mind of an official faced with a strong ministerial desire to set an overstretching target. On one side of a set of scales inside your head is your discomfort at conspiring in an unduly optimistic schedule. On the other is a stack of weighty considerations encouraging you to do so. These start with a genuine professional desire to serve the duly appointed minister of a democratically elected government. In the case of Universal Credit, you are also likely to be personally attracted to the policy objectives. The upside of rationalising the benefits system had been talked about in the Department for years; now there was finally a ministerial team that was up for the challenge. Calling into question the deliverability of the policy would lead to delay at best, and might even risk the survival of the whole project. It would certainly embolden the project's enemies inside and outside of government. On the other hand, going forward on an aggressive schedule might drive momentum into delivery, and then who knows what might be achieved? These selfless incentives are joined by a less altruistic one. Acknowledging reality can be perilous for your career. So why not find a way to bury the risks and uncertainties in the small print and hope for the best? You can comfort yourself that those around you also seem supportive of the schedule. The likelihood of you being personally held to account for your advice is low, and anyway you will be in a different job within a year or two.

No one is incentivised to probe too deeply into whether the promise is actually deliverable.

*

Whatever else Universal Credit has achieved, it has not solved the problem of how to encourage welfare recipients to become more economically active. Uniquely amongst the G7 nations, in 2024, UK employment still lagged its pre-pandemic level, and the number who are not working on the grounds of ill-health had risen steeply. After the election, Labour's incoming Work and Pensions Secretary, Liz Kendall, was quick to blame her Tory predecessors' fixation with Universal Credit.

> DWP was focused almost entirely on the benefits system. And specifically on implementing Universal Credit. JobcentrePlus [has become] a benefit monitoring service, not a public employment service – which was its original aim. Nowhere near enough attention [is paid] to the wider issues – like health, skills, childcare, transport – that play such a huge role in determining whether you get work, stay in work and get on in your work. The result is a system that is too siloed and too centralised.[17]

Her declared prescription was a new jobs and careers service, guaranteed training or a job for those entering adulthood, and devolution of more power to mayors and local government. Time will tell what role Universal Credit will play in Labour's plans.

6

COMPLEXITY: SMART METERS

I probably wouldn't have admitted it at the time, but to be honest, I was nervous. It was the day of my first appearance in front of the Energy and Climate Change Select Committee. Even old hands take providing evidence to Select Committees seriously, but if you slip-up as a rookie like me it can follow you around for years.

We were seated in one of the light-green committee rooms in Portcullis House, across the road from Parliament. The committee of MPs was arranged in a horseshoe in front of me, and there were banks of chairs at my back for officials and interested members of the public. But if they hadn't been able to make it, they could always have watched it live on the BBC's Parliament channel, as I knew my team back at the office was going to do.

I was there because I was running something called the Data and Communication Company, DCC, a private sector company charged with providing the new national communications infrastructure which was going to link 50 million new smart meters with the energy companies which supplied them. Sitting beside me was Sacha Deshmukh. He was there because it was his job promote to the public the idea of having their old analogue electricity and gas meters replaced by new digital smart meters. Sasha looked confident and relaxed, but I was feeling the pressure. That was because in 2010 the then Energy Minister Charles Hendry had announced that the DCC infrastructure, and the IT systems that were needed to run it, would be available in the autumn of 2013, thereby allowing every property to become smart by 2020. Now it was December 2014, and I still couldn't tell the committee when we would be ready.

Although the Smart Meter project had its detractors, everyone in the project knew that once we got to the stage of deploying millions of meters into people's homes, then stopping the project would be close to impossible. But if the Government had a crisis of confidence before that point then we might all be out of a job. An incompetent performance in front of a Select Committee wouldn't help. So my task was to sound confident and competent, but without making any promises that I didn't know we could keep. With members of my team, I had been practicing the answers to some very hard questions. My main hope was that Sacha's area of the project would prove to be more interesting to the MPs than my lack of progress with the infrastructure. Sacha was more experienced with politicians than I was, but I knew he had been rehearsing too.

But we really needn't have bothered. Despite having a staff of researchers and several days of hearings at their disposal, the MPs didn't really seem to understand what the project was all about. The Chair, Tim Yeo, started off aggressively enough. 'Given that the National Grid and the distribution companies run rings around Ofgem on a routine basis and make considerable excess profits, what will happen if you do the same thing?'[1] I began to explain how the remuneration of DCC was calculated, but he had made his point and wasn't going to tolerate a long explanation. Instead, he wanted to know how I was going to solve the problem of installing smart meters in tower blocks. I tried to explain that it was the Energy Suppliers who were going to install the meters rather than me, but I found myself struggling to get the point across. 'That is a very long way of saying you do not have a solution and you are quite happy to wash your hands of the problem' he said. And so it went on.

An hour and 80 mis-fired questions later, the committee members had lost interest in me and had moved on to Sacha. But by that stage, they were not so much waving at the Smart Meter project as drowning in its complexity. Peter Lilley had the floor. 'Say this is my smart meter in my kitchen here, can I look at it and use it to shop or do I have to go to the web?' Sasha began to explain how smart metering would allow switching services like uSwitch to help consumers get the best deal available. The MP was confused. 'But explain how you do it. I tap into what? I have this machine on my desk – actually I have already lost the machine... but forget about that. Supposing I had not lost it, and I still have it. What would I have to tap into it to do one of these price comparisons?' Foolishly, I thought I could help Sacha out. 'You are not going to use your in-home display for this...'. 'So that is completely useless?' I wasn't sure he was following. The confused grilling went on for another thirty minutes until the Committee Chair gratefully called time and the MPs trooped off for lunch.

For Parliament, a Select Committee should be just about the best way of holding government to account. The Institute for Government says that they should 'allow MPs and peers to develop a degree of specialisation in a subject, encouraging deeper and more effective scrutiny of the government'.[2] In the Smart Meter project, we were on the verge of beginning a roll-out that would cost consumers an estimated £11 billion. And at the last, best chance of scrutinising the project before it passed the point of no return, the Committee simply didn't understand what the government was doing. None of us did a particularly good morning's work that day, but this isn't just an anecdote about how some Select Committee members don't do their homework and are more interested in grandstanding than understanding. A better committee might still have been confused. The truth is that what we were doing was very, very confusing.

It didn't have to be this complex.

At its simplest, there were two metering problems facing governments in the new millennium. The first was that the old analogue electricity meters, which had hardly changed in a hundred years, couldn't be read remotely. That meant that the bill a consumer pays had to be estimated. For most consumers, the same problem applied to their gas meters. In the digital age, this is not ideal. Every developed country faced this problem, although the UK could have joined those, like Germany, who appeared content to live with the status quo.

But the second problem would have been harder to ignore. In the country's electricity generation and distribution infrastructure, a revolution was underway. Historically, the country had always had an electricity network dominated by a small number of large coal, oil, nuclear and natural gas generators which fed electricity into the grid. From there, it was distributed through networks of cables to consumers. Power flows were monitored at regional and local levels, but exactly where the electricity was consumed was not very important for managing the grid. There was no need for real-time consumption data even at a suburb level, let alone home by home. But now, generation from wind and solar was beginning to happen all over the place, including in domestic dwellings. To manage an electricity grid in this new world needs real-time data – lots of it.

And there was another problem. The electricity network has to work when the sun isn't shining and the wind isn't blowing. That means that as well as wind turbines and solar panels, the country will need a mix of large new generators and energy storage facilities. Whether nuclear, gas generators with carbon capture, or hydro-electric, this is going to be very expensive. Just how expensive depends on whether consumers can be encouraged to reduce peak consumption, which in turn requires near-term data about consumption at the household level. Evangelists for a smart energy grid will describe to you a world in which smart devices in your home automatically respond to price signals by trimming back consumption and using the batteries in your electric car to power the house. Reducing peak consumption, they will tell you, will not only save you money on your electricity bill, but will save the country billions in investment in new electricity generation, distribution and storage. And you can't do any of this without smart electricity meters.

The need for smart metering has been understood in the electricity sector for decades. Smart meter trials were announced in the Blair government's 2006 budget. The following year, Alistair Darling, the Secretary of State in the Department for Trade and Industry, presented a White Paper proposing the installation of meters to all houses within a decade, and the policy development for a smart meter project began.[3]

At its simplest, a smart meter implementation project could have worked like this. Your old analogue meter would be replaced by a modern electricity meter with a communication device, like a SIM card, which would transmit your consumption data over a mobile network (referred to as the Wide Area Network) to the energy company. This would allow accurate billing and provide the data needed to modernise the grid. And as for the replacement of the physical meter, it would have been done by one of the eight regional companies that operate the electrical distribution network. They would have procured the meters and contracted with a suitable telecommunication provider in their region. You could imagine installation being done town by town, street by street, across the land over a number of years. I can just about remember, in the 60s and 70s, when this was exactly the way that the regional gas boards modified all the gas appliances in the country as we switched from town gas to natural gas. It is also the way that other countries have approached the problem. A smart meter project like this would be big and expensive, but relatively simple.

But in the UK, the Government decided to do something much, much more complex. Great Britain has a curious electricity market, in which your energy supplier is not the company who supplies your energy. Almost everywhere else in the world, a household's energy supplier is the private or public utility which owns the cables which run to your house. But when electricity was privatised in Great Britain in the 1990s, the bit of the system which owns the infrastructure was separated from the bit that sells and bills you for electricity. That was because the infrastructure is a natural monopoly and successive governments believed in the benefits of competition. So a monopoly network operator provides the electricity to your home, but a competitive market place of energy suppliers compete for your business of paying for it. This isn't the place for an argument about whether this was a good idea, but it certainly makes the electricity business complicated. It means that every house in your street could have a different electricity supplier, and next year they could all be different again, as customers switch suppliers looking for a better deal. So in the simple smart meter roll-out I described above, there would inevitably be a complication. The regional network operator who remotely read your meter would have to provide the relevant Energy Supplier with the consumption data for billing.

Even with this complication, a Smart Meter project could have been a large but relatively simple endeavour. But what actually happened as the project developed was that at every decision point, faced with a choice between simplicity and complexity, the project chose the more complex option. In each case, the decisions were driven by theoretical benefits. There was always a good reason why the complicated answer was a better answer. But the result was a project of byzantine complexity. Even telling the story is complicated, but the most consequential decisions could be summarised as follows.

Firstly, rather than conceiving of the project as an upgrade of the nation's energy infrastructure, led by the eight regional network operators for the benefit of all, it was, from the beginning, conceived as being led by consumers for their own individual advantage. Rather than looking for the most cost-effective way of installing smart meters to provide accurate bills and to support modernising the grid, the project presented itself as being about delivering immediate benefits for the consumer. Thus, it was decided, the installation of meters would be undertaken not by the network operators, but by the energy suppliers. This apparently simple decision had huge implications. It meant that any idea of rolling out street by street became impractical, since each street, while having a single network operator, would have many suppliers. Instead, each consumer would have to be individually convinced to have a smart meter, including those who don't want one or don't speak English, and those who think that any communications network really exists to facilitate the deep-state spying on them. So each supplier had to absorb the inefficiency of installing meters randomly across the country. But the main complexity that supplier-led installation created was how to allow a consumer who received a new meter from Supplier A in January to switch to Supplier B in February. This meant, firstly, that every supplier's smart meter had to be able to operate with every other supplier's IT systems. That in turn meant that every supplier had to sign up to a new set of rules that would define how all this interoperability would work. It was called the Smart Energy Code. This document, which describes everybody's obligations and responsibilities, runs to an extraordinary 2,319 pages.

Furthermore, interoperability means that every supplier has to use the same data and telecommunications infrastructure. So, ironically, in the interests of competition, it was necessary to provide a new national infrastructure monopoly. It was this service, which became known as the Data and Communications Company, DCC, that I found myself running in 2013 and which put me in front of the Energy Select Committee at the end of 2014.

The focus on maximising immediate benefits for householders, rather than the electricity system as a whole, also led to the inclusion of gas meters. This may seem perfectly logical, but it also had big consequences for the project. Now, as well as having a smart electricity meter which could communicate with any energy supplier across a Wide Area Network, you also needed a new secure wireless network within the home, the Home Area Network, which allowed the new smart gas meter to communicate with the new smart electricity meter. And, of course, the consumer cannot really take control of their consumption if it requires them to look under the stairs for the electricity meter reading and in the garage for the gas meter reading. So the home also had to be provided with a display device linked to both the meters to show consumption. This new Home Area Network adds yet another layer of complexity to the project. It also raises a problem for blocks of flats, where the electricity meter may be on the fifteenth floor and the gas meter in the basement.

So, to summarise, instead of eight large but simple smart electricity meter projects run by the regional network operators, this project required each of the dozens of electricity suppliers to work with a new market of electricity and gas meter manufacturers whose completely interoperable meters had to be able to communicate across a new type of Home Area Network, to a brand new national data and communication monopoly, DCC, which had contracts with telecommunication companies to provide a Wide Area Network. And all this had to be bound together by an immense new regulatory framework.

Before I lose you completely, there is one final decision to mention. While all of this policy was under development, a minority of the energy suppliers were keen to begin rolling out smart meters to their existing customers, without waiting for a national DCC infrastructure and the development of a smart energy code to allow interoperability. If there had been a value placed on simplicity, the government's response would have been to require them to wait. But government could see the advantage of having some experimentation and innovation. Here was a chance for suppliers to learn about rolling out meters, and for at least some customers to begin to get used to the idea of having a smart meter. Yes, there would be a problem later because these first-generation meters would not be interoperable with the rest, meaning that if a customer changed energy supplier then their smart meter would go dumb again, but the numbers were expected to be very small. Two things helped this small problem to grow into a big and expensive problem. The first was that the energy regulator began placing obligations on all suppliers to begin rolling out these first-generation meters. The second was that agreeing the Smart Energy Code, and creating a brand new highly secure national data and communications infrastructure and the meters to communicate across it, took much much longer than hoped. So the number of first-generation meters had time to grow until, eventually, finding a way to make them interoperable became a huge and difficult technical issue. In fact, it is likely that millions of them will have to be replaced with compliant meters at great expense.

Now, just to be clear, all of these individual policy choices were driven by what, on the face of it, looked like genuine benefits. It *would* be a good thing if consumers took control of their energy use and reduced consumption. It *would* be good to be able to remotely read gas-meters. It *wasn't* a bad idea to let the energy suppliers experiment with first-generation meters. The problem is that each choice added complexity to the project. Eight large but relatively simple projects became a single, huge, expensive and enormously complex project. And the problem with hugely complex projects is that they never, ever, proceed as expected. They always take a lot longer and cost a lot more.

The 2010 announcement by Energy Minister Hendry – the one which I was so worried about before the Select Committee meeting – had announced that the DCC would be set up by mid-2012 and its infrastructure would be fully tested by autumn 2013.[4] This would allow seven years to complete the roll-out of meters before the target of 2020. Because of the complexities just described, this proved to be hopelessly optimistic. The competition to procure someone to set up the DCC took a year longer than planned, and getting the infrastructure working took three years longer. But even when we in the DCC were ready, at the end of 2016, none of the smart meter manufacturers had yet been able to produce a reliable meter that would cope with all the complexities of interoperability. So the rollout began at a snail's pace and only really gained momentum towards the end of the decade.

The proportion of meters that are smart crept past 50% sometime during 2022, although many of these are first-generation meters which are no longer operating in smart mode. The target for completion has slipped several times. The current plan is to have smart meters installed in 80% of homes by the beginning of 2026. It is a good bet that the full roll-out will take a decade longer than originally hoped.

Counterfactuals are treacherous, but I think it is reasonable to say that a simpler smart meter project – one focussed on electricity meters and rolled out as an energy infrastructure project rather than a consumer-driven behavioural change project – could have completed a decade earlier, at much lower cost. And it would not have required the creation of a complex new piece of national data and communications infrastructure with thousands of pages of new regulation. It is true that it wouldn't have been able to claim all the consumer benefits that the actual project is targeting, but the reality is that benefits only flow from delivery, not from aspirational business cases. And who knows what innovative energy solutions might have been built in the 2020s on the back of a simple, but successful, roll-out of smart electricity meters.

*

I have used the word 'complexity' a number of times to describe what went wrong in the Smart Meter project, but what is it? Project complexity defies simple definition, but some of the characteristics of the Smart Meter project give a sense of how it manifests itself.

If your project is highly bespoke and there is no existing class of similar projects against which to gauge its feasibility, then it is complex. If you have to start implementation before you really know what you are doing, that's complex. If you have to develop a new supply chain, transform an existing one, or encourage a lot of players to work together in a completely new way, despite their different objectives and commercial drivers, that's complex. If you aim for universality, meeting the needs of everyone, including the vulnerable, the conspiratorial, the confused, and the unwilling, then that's complex.

So complexity in major projects means more than just 'very complicated'. Every large project is complicated, with many moving parts that require a lot of coordinating. All the techniques of modern project management – planning, scheduling, risk analysis, change control – have developed to cope with this kind of complication. But some projects tip over from complication to complexity, which makes delivering them to a predictable timeline and cost essentially impossible. Crossrail trains required unique on-board software to switch seamlessly between three separate signalling systems. This required what Mark Wild told me was 'probably the most complicated train ever made'. No one could have said in advance how long it would take to integrate all those systems and get them to work together.[5] The Home Office project to provide mobile communications for the blue-light services, even though it was trying to achieve something that every developed country is already doing, managed to develop into what someone close to the project described as 'the most complex telecoms project ever undertaken'. Universal Credit required parts of government to work together in a new way in order to serve an infinitely diverse population of claimants through a completely new IT architecture delivered through a new project methodology. Even if ministers had wanted a realistic assessment of how long it would take, which they didn't, the level of uncertainty at the beginning was so large that the only honest answer to the question of when it would be finished would have been 'who knows'.

So why do so many government projects fall into the complexity trap?

In the case of the Smart Meter project, it was not as if the complexity wasn't recognised from the outset. Ministers and officials took pride in it. In 2009, Ed Milliband's Department of Energy and Climate Change cheerily described their Smart Meter proposals, then still on the drawing board, as being 'the largest and most complex such deployment anywhere in the world'.[6] That should have set off a loud alarm bell. Why didn't it?

Between the Labour Government's first White Paper in 2007 and the formal launch of the project in 2010, there were five Ministers of State for Energy. Since 2010 there have been 13 more. So for ministers, the immediate political upside of a racy project announcement will always trump the long-term risks of actually delivering it. If your tenure is likely to be less than a year, then why would you put yourself in the position of having to explain that your project was not going to cover gas meters? Why not squeeze every last potential benefit from a project you are never going to be held to account for? But this isn't the whole answer. Smart meters are not the most politically exciting subject in the world. No minister was promoted because they insisted on including gas-meters in the smart meter roll-out. No Special Advisor devoted their short time in government to forcing the early adoption of first-generation meters. Electricity and gas meters just aren't that sexy. Ministers announced what was put in front of them by policy civil servants.

So here is the first reason that such a complex approach was taken. Policy civil servants are really comfortable with complexity. They have to be. The challenges facing a modern developed state are intrinsically complex. You need really clever people to address them. Recruitment into the civil service fast stream deliberately targets big brains that can absorb complexity and tolerate ambiguity. Recruitment literature *promises* 'projects of unparalleled complexity'. In short, the smart meter policy team was much more comfortable with theoretically perfect complexity than judgemental and pragmatic realism. What made this problem worse was that the project in its early years was surrounded by people incentivised to downplay the impact of complexity. Dozens of consultants were employed by the Department and the energy regulator to develop the regulatory regime. The IT companies servicing the energy sector were particularly incentivised. Firstly, the project was so large that they couldn't risk missing out by admitting how hard it was going to be. And secondly, as in all complex projects, the government's requirements were bound to change, which meant that the bidders were not taking much real risk in their bids. I wasn't immune from these motivations. My colleagues and I won the competition to become the Data Communication Company by presenting the most reassuring case we could about how we would manage the roll-out. Nobody had an incentive to say that a simpler project could have avoided the need for the DCC altogether.

The final piece of the puzzle is the way government ranks options for how a policy objective can be delivered. Just like in the private sector, the idea is to choose the option with the highest ratio of benefits to costs. The problem is that the benefits of a complex solution are shiny, popular, and easy to quantify. But the extent of the almost inevitable consequences of complexity – delay and cost growth – can't be predicted with accuracy. When you put this reality together with the incentives in the system, the option analysis will always favour the complex over the simple. You can see this starkly in the Department's 2010 communication about the forthcoming project. In the same report that declared that the project would be the most complex in the world, they also promised to 'ensure the roll-out is implemented in a way which minimises cost and risk ... and delivers the maximum benefits'.[7] It sounds like an anodyne objective; the lowest cost, the lowest risk, and the highest benefits. But a project which really minimised cost and risk would have been radically simpler. It would have delivered a narrower set of benefits and be well over by now. Instead, chasing all the theoretically available benefits had the consequence of evolving a project which would postpone delivery of any benefits at all for years and years.

*

There is no denying that most problems that major government projects are intended to address have a level of intrinsic complexity. In fact, the National Audit Office has developed a tool for measuring complexity. It's called the DECA – Delivery Environment Complexity Analytic – and it is advocated by the Cabinet Office as the best way to understand how complex your project is.[8] But the response to complexity is always the same: more resource, more reporting, more governance, and more assurance. The Cabinet Office's manual on setting up projects for success has well over a hundred references to complexity – but not a single mention of simplification.[9]

One of the best ways to avoid kicking off a doomed project is to simplify it into a deliverable one. That might be as simple as designing the policy with implementation firmly in mind, or breaking down the delivery into independent chunks. But if the chunks aren't actually independent then your plan may *look* simpler, but you have probably made it much less likely to deliver. The Smart Meter project was indeed split into separate parts, but the parts were anything but independent. The regulator, energy suppliers, network operators, telecoms companies, meter manufacturers and the DCC itself were all dependent on each other. And they all had to finish on time for the project to succeed. The problem with this is simple mathematics. Even if every one of the component projects was 80% likely to succeed, then the end-to-end service would only have had a 25% chance of being complete on time. And none of the components in the British Smart Meter project had anything like an 80% chance of delivering on time. Failure was inevitable.

If we want less failed major government projects, this is one of the most important lessons we have to learn. The very first question about a complex project should not be how to deal with its complexity – but how to dramatically reduce it. And if proceeding with real complexity can't be avoided, then don't expect the project to go according to plan. And don't promise that it will.

I have three more failures to describe. The first is a project that couldn't be simplified. There is no such thing as a simple nuclear submarine.

7

THE INVERSE SQUARE LAW: ASTUTE

On 18th March 1997, front pages were dominated by the impeding general election. The Tory party was unpopular and divided and Labour was widely expected to win, but since John Major's unexpected victory in 1992, nobody was taking anything for granted. The speculation of the day was whether Tony Blair would risk his lead in a head-to-head television election debate, which if it happened would be the first in British history. But buried in the inner pages of the *Financial Times* was a shorter story: 'GEC wins £2bn submarine contract'.[1] The reporter, citing Ministry of Defence sources, said that GEC had won the contract partly 'because of its innovative production methods, involving plans for modular assembly of the 6,000 tonne submarines, and the superior nuclear power technology offered by its subcontractors'. This milestone, greeted with enormous relief in GEC Marconi after a prolonged procurement process, was in fact the start of one of the most calamitous projects ever carried out by the MoD.

The Astute project was set up to produce the next generation of nuclear-powered attack submarines. The first, HMS *Astute*, should have gone into service in 2005, to begin replacing the Swiftsure class, which would by then have been in service for 32 years and ready to retire. Even the newer Trafalgar class submarines would be 22 years old by then and the new Astute boats would be badly needed. But it actually took until 2013 for HMS *Astute* to go into service. As of summer 2024, with the Swiftsure class long ago decommissioned and the last of the Trafalgar class due to go out of service in 2025, only five of the seven Astute class submarines have been commissioned and the last, HMS *Agincourt*, is still years away. The original intention was that in the 2020s, there should be a dozen attack submarines in the fleet. Because of the time it has taken to build the Astute class, the actual number is not 12, but 6.

The seeds of the failure had been sown long before the contract was awarded in 1997. The thousands of professionals who have tried to rescue the Astute project since then have failed to overcome a series of disastrous decisions taken by the government well before the first welding arc was struck in the shipyard. To understand what happened, you need to know a little about the UK's nuclear submarines.

*

Every hour of every day, there is at least one trident armed nuclear submarine lurking silently at sea, providing the ultimate deterrent to the nation's adversaries. The UK's Continuous At-Sea Deterrent CASD, has been the cornerstone of the nation's defence strategy for well over half a century. The Royal Navy calls it Operation Relentless. Nuclear submariners call it 'the tip of the spear'. To guarantee CASD, the Navy always has four submarines capable of carrying nuclear weapons in commission. The current 'deterrent' boats, known as the Vanguard class, will be replaced in the 2030s by the Dreadnought class, currently under construction in Barrow in Furness in Cumbria. Deterrent submarines are protected by so-called 'attack' submarines. Smaller and faster, the attack submarine's role is to safeguard the deterrent and to hunt for the submarines of the UK's potential adversaries.

When the contract for HMS *Astute* was announced in 1997, construction was well advanced on the fourth and last of the Vanguard class deterrent submarines, HMS *Vengeance*. At the time, these submarines were, without doubt, the most complex feat of engineering ever undertaken in Britain. A quarter of a century later, they probably still are. Each boat is a nuclear power station contained within a self-propelling metal tube. It operates hidden for months in one of the least hospitable environments on earth,

providing a home for over a hundred submariners. It manufac-
tures its own fresh air and water, and stores enough food for six
months submerged. While on patrol, the boat must remain completely undetectable to its adversaries. Its mechanical plant is close
to silent, and its crew move soundlessly about their duties to avoid
the noise of their footfall being carried out into the ocean. When on
patrol it is utterly alone. The captain, who will always be a gradu-
ate of the world-famous 'Perisher' training course, is responsible
for every aspect of the patrol, with extremely limited communication with the outside world.

Designing, building and maintaining nuclear submarines
requires a unique combination of capabilities. And for reasons of
national security, everything has to be sourced and manufactured in
the UK. The nations with the industrial weight to sustain a nuclear
submarine fleet make up a very small club. It is no coincidence that
for the first 60 years of nuclear submarines the only nations with
the capability were the 5 permanent members of the UN Security
Council. They have recently been joined by India.

Remarkably, in the 34 years before the keel was laid on HMS
Vengeance, the Barrow dockyard had constructed 24 new nuclear
submarines – one every 17 months on average. In this context, the
failure of the Astute project is staggering. Astute's predecessors, the
7 Trafalgar class boats, were constructed, launched and commissioned in around 12.5 years. For the same number of boats, the
Astute project will take at least 25. And in submarine building,
time is money. There is a saying in the shipyard: 'The way to build
a very expensive boat is... slowly'.

Underlying the failure of the Astute project is a phenomenon common to many major government projects, whereby appreciation of
the difficulty of delivery is inversely proportional to how far you are
from it. From two steps away, a submarine project looks four times
easier than it really is. And those three steps away, in Whitehall, just
can't see how it can possibly take so long and cost so much. And
if these are the people deciding when and how the next generation
of submarines are to be built, then the inverse square law can drive
decisions which look, in retrospect, spectacularly naive.

The first case of the inverse square law as applied to the Astute
project was the failure to recognise, in the centre of government

and in the MoD, that if they were not used, then the unique capabilities required to design and build nuclear submarines would
begin to atrophy and erode.[2] Decisions about what kind of a submarine should replace the Trafalgar class – how big, how fast, how
capable and how quiet – were needed by the mid-1980s if the naval
architects and designers coming off the Vanguard class design were
to be retained for the next generation of attack submarines. This
would have allowed the first orders to be placed early in the 1990s
and would have had the first boat in-service by the millennium.[3] As
the Navy's initial studies into the successor to the Trafalgar class
got under way, there was no end to the Cold War in sight. Military
capability was the driving requirement, and cost was a secondary
consideration. The early plan for what became the Astute class was
for a completely new submarine, which had little in common with
Trafalgar. Powered by the same nuclear plant as the new Vanguard
class, it would be capable of more speed and greater depth than
Trafalgar. It would be a large and expensive submarine. But by
the end of the decade, the Iron Curtain had fallen, and the Sovi-
et Union was heading for collapse. As the Cold War came to an
end, the UK and its allies began to look for a peace dividend. This
changed the balance of priorities for the next generation of attack
submarines away from capability and towards cost. In 1990, the
decision was taken to abandon the idea of a completely new submarine and instead to modernise and update the Trafalgar class
design. The boat design was given the working title of B2TC –
Batch 2 Trafalgar class.

As the debate about what kind of submarine should replace the
Trafalgar class dragged on, the start of detailed design drifted back-
wards and the projected date for the first boat entering service moved
into the 2000s. The Navy could accommodate the delay because the
more modern submarines were lasting longer than earlier classes.
And in response to the lower threat from Russia, the Navy reduced
its attack submarine fleet from 18 to 15 and the MoD was anticipat-
ing further reductions down to around 12. All of this meant that as
the oldest of the Swiftsure class submarines began to reach the end of
their lives, they didn't need to be replaced straight away.

But while the Navy could survive without new submarines, the
submarine delivery machine at the shipyard couldn't. By the time

the detailed design of the B2TC submarine began, it was nearly 20 years since the design of the Vanguard class and the gap between laying down HMS *Vengeance* and HMS *Astute* was 8 years. The shipyard owners, Vickers Shipbuilding and Engineering Ltd (VSEL) had to drastically reduce the workforce and try desperately to pick up other work to keep the shipyard open. From a peak of 13,000 employees during the Vanguard Programme, the workforce dropped to around 3,000. The engineers, designers and tradesmen who had sustained the 17-month drumbeat of new nuclear submarines through the seventies and eighties melted away. The remaining workforce was employed on building whatever surface ship contracts VSEL could bring in. This meant that when design work on B2TC was intended to start, most of the depleted design workforce was already tied up on other work. The capability to build nuclear submarines in Barrow in Furness, the nation's only shipyard with any experience of the task, had been allowed to atrophy and then die. The inverse square law meant that no-one in Whitehall had realised that this remote corner of Cumbria nurtured a unique national asset. And no-one recognised the consequences for the nation's ability to sustain a nuclear submarine fleet for the future. The capability to build submarines at the required rate has not yet recovered. This is the inverse square law at work. But it wasn't the only example of the law in the Astute project.

The MoD had always played the commanding role in the design and production of nuclear submarines. While the detailed design and construction of the boats was done by VSEL at the Barrow Shipyard, and of the nuclear reactors by Rolls-Royce in Derby, all the overall design decisions were made by the MoD under the leadership of the Director General Submarines, generally a Rear Admiral level naval officer. The MoD was what is known as the Design Authority. Based in Bath, where they had been evacuated from London during the War, the Royal Corps of Naval Constructors were in charge of the overall design. Their job was to make sure that all of the individual systems that make up a nuclear submarine would integrate into something that would survive in the unique environment of long, lonely, silent patrols. This body of professionals, made up of experienced Royal Navy officers and civil servants, naval architects and engineers, could trace its history back to Tudor times. The Navy also oversaw the detailed design and construction work undertaken in the Shipyard through the watchful eye of an experienced officer known as the Principal Naval Overseer and a small army of engineers. They checked that what was being built was what was required, and had the authority to approve the kind of minor design changes that are always needed when you try to bring a hugely complex accumulation of plant together into a finished submarine. When it came to testing and commissioning, it was another naval officer, the Captain of Submarine Acceptance, who oversaw the process and made the ultimate decision as to whether the boat had been built with sufficient quality to allow it to go to sea. This was the tried and tested way to build nuclear submarines.

But it isn't how most defence equipment is procured. In general, for surface ships, aircraft, and armoured vehicles, the MoD outsources the role of Design Authority to industry. The MoD specifies its functional requirements – how big, how fast and with what firepower – but the prime contractor is responsible for turning these requirements into a design specification and making sure that the equipment fulfils them. The risk that the product doesn't meet the functional specification is, at least in theory, transferred to industry. It is their job to make sure it works. Viewed from the distance of Whitehall, in accordance with the inverse square law, it seemed obvious in the 1990s that what was good enough for an aeroplane or a ship would be good enough for a nuclear submarine. So government decided that the prime contractor would be the Design Authority in the B2TC project. This meant that the withering of capability that had happened in the shipyard was also underway in Bath. The Royal Corps of Naval Constructors stopped recruiting, and the Ministry's role in the shipyard became an approach referred to as 'eyes on – hands off', although in practice there were fewer and fewer 'eyes on'. The Principal Naval Overseer role was abandoned, as was the Captain Submarine Acceptance. The government's presence in the shipyard reduced almost to nothing. This fundamental change to the way submarines were to be built was imposed without any planning about how to mitigate its risks. It was just assumed that industry would step up to the accountabilities previously owned by the Ministry.

If the first example of the inverse square law was the failure to recognise that submarine building was a nationally important capability which would disappear if not exercised, and the second was to believe that the role of Design Authority and construction overseer could be passed over to industry without consequences, then the third was the assumption that the best way to get cheaper, better, submarines was to hold an open competition.

In the mid-1980s, the Defence Secretary, Michael Heseltine, had insisted that the MoD hire his special advisor Peter Levene to the role of Chief of Defence Procurement. Levene held the role into the 1990s. Heseltine had been convinced that the 'national champion' defence suppliers were ripping off the government 'in spades', because they were awarded projects unopposed, and their costs were reimbursed through 'cost-plus' contracts.[4] Heseltine and Levene believed that the answer was to run competitions for everything and to award fixed price contracts. Levene described his philosophy in his autobiography: never accept the first price from industry. even if it is the lowest price bid in the competition.

> I introduced what I called 'the Levene Law' which meant that every potential contract was sent back to the negotiating table three or four times. By 1998 this had produced several cases where tender prices had mysteriously dropped by up to 30% in the bidding rounds.[5]

So even though the Vanguard boats had been delivered to cost, the government was convinced that VSEL were making excessive profits without taking any risk. For the B2TC project, competition would break this cosy arrangement and a fixed price contract would transfer the delivery risk to the winning firm. The government fostered the development of a consortium, led by GEC Marconi, to go up against VSEL. In case GEC Marconi were put off by the cost of bidding against the firm who had built all the British nuclear submarines in living memory, the government decided to reimburse the cost of bidding. An invitation to tender was issued in July 1994. The competition would cover the design of the B2TC, including being the Design Authority, and delivery of the first three boats.

Because GEC Marconi had no muscle memory from delivering previous submarines, the MoD had to specify, in the competition, not just the performance requirements that the submarine would have to meet, but also a vast number of very specific technical requirements. So having decided as a matter of principle to pass the Design Authority to industry, the MoD now over-specified the details in a way that removed the Design Authority's ability to make its own decisions. The consequence was that the contractor could never be really held accountable for the boat's design.

Understandably, VSEL made a bid to build the B2TC submarines pretty much the way it had learnt to do over the decades. They also included costs to cover rebuilding the submarine-specific capability that had been allowed to erode over the years since HMS *Vanguard* had been designed. But the MoD thought the VSEL bid was unambitious, conservative and boring. The GEC Marconi bid, by contrast, seemed exciting, innovative and modern. Their plan was to build the boats in sections at various shipyards around England, creating new jobs in a number of depressed areas. They claimed it would also lead to lower wage costs. The sections would then be shipped to the Devonport Dockyard in Plymouth where the final submarines would be assembled. GEC Marconi's final innovation, which promised great efficiencies and fewer errors, was the use of three-dimensional computer aided design, 3D-CAD. It is hard to believe now, but previous submarine designs had been produced by hundreds of draughtsmen at drawing boards using pencil, pen and ink. Integration of designs across the whole boat had been done my making huge wooden mock-ups of the submarine sections, so that designers could check that pipe x wasn't going to block walkway y. Computer-aided design was not completely new. It had been used for surface ships. But it had never been used on anything as complicated and crowded as the interior of a nuclear submarine. The time saving that GEC Marconi promised 3D-CAD would bring was the cherry on the top of their bid.

In June 1995, in the middle of the bidding process, the Ministry's strategy of competition suffered a major set-back. GEC Marconi bought VSEL. Now the government was inviting competing bids from two parts of the same company. Determined to maintain a competition, the MoD insisted GEC Marconi had to keep the two bidding teams separate. So, while there was no longer any doubt that GEC Marconi would win the competition, the bidding team bringing the innovation in the competition was not allowed to benefit from the experience of the only shipyard that had built a nuclear submarine in decades – even though they were part of the same company. By the end of the year, the MoD had concluded that the GEC Marconi bid was cheaper and more innovative than the ex-VSEL bid, and the Company was informed that of their two bids, this one was preferred. But there was still a problem. Both tenders significantly exceeded the Ministry's available budget. So they deployed the latest version of 'Levene's Law', which was known as NAPNoC – No Acceptable Price – No Contract. In other words – reduce your price or there will be no deal. The MoD produced its own estimate of what it thought B2TC submarines should cost and began extensive negotiations to convince GEC Marconi to accept a fixed price that was within the MoD's affordability window. The company had by now realised that building the boats in Barrow was by far the best option, and as the only remaining bidder they were not prepared to accept a simple fixed price. Instead, what was negotiated was a target price, and a gain-share pain-share arrangement. If the final cost was a pound below the target, MoD would pocket 70p and GEC Marconi 30p. And if the costs went the other way, then MoD would pay 70% of the additional cost. But GEC Marconi was forced to agree to a maximum price, beyond which they would have to pay every penny. The final part of the deal was to agree milestones against which payments would be made during the construction period. The contractor would receive payment when predefined volumes of steel, pipework, cables and so on were installed.

These difficult negotiations took the whole of 1996 and into 1997. In the middle of the negotiations, the position of Chief of Defence Procurement at the MoD was given to Sir Robert Walmsley, an experienced ex-submariner who had just retired at the rank of Vice-Admiral in the Royal Navy. Walmsley was certainly not subject to the inverse square law. He knew exactly how difficult it would be to build the B2TC submarines. But he was also deeply committed to the submarine service and needed to get the project going. Everyone knew that the Labour party, which, despite its modernising leadership, had advocated unilateral nuclear disarmament as recently as the previous decade, was likely to win the forthcoming general election. If the contracts were not signed by election day, then at best there would be a delay, and at worst the whole project could be kicked into the long grass until a Strategic Defence Review was completed. So both the MoD and GEC Marconi really wanted to strike a deal before the election, and it was this contract that was signed in March 1997.

The MoD was convinced it had got what it needed. They had run a competition, which had forced fresh thinking and innovation. They had capped the maximum price, transferred a lot of risk to the private sector, and got a contract that promised delivery of the first boat eight years later in 2005. Although five years later than originally intended, the date could be accommodated by the Navy because the new Defence Secretary, Labour's George Robertson, did indeed undertake a Strategic Defence Review after the election. One of its decisions was to plan a further reduction in the size of the attack submarine fleet, down from twelve to ten boats.

Early on, the MoD thought the project was going well, but in reality, as the design got underway, the inverse square law was beginning to bite. Lacking experience, GEC Marconi didn't understand how badly things were going. It was almost 20 years since the Vanguard class design had begun and much of what little corporate memory was left in VSEL had been lost in the acquisition. And the MoD was even more unsighted. There were now just two naval officers and two civil servants in the shipyard. Without the MoD playing its project management, Design Authority, and integration roles, and with the loss of VSEL's shipyard experience, it was as though every challenge was being faced for the first time.

As the second batch of the Trafalgar class, B2TC was supposed to be a low-risk proposition. But early design decisions quickly took the boat, now renamed the Astute class, further and further away from the Trafalgar class. The biggest decision was to design the new attack class with the same nuclear reactor that had been used in the Vanguard ballistic class boats. These were more powerful than the reactors in previous attack submarines and had the huge benefit that they could last the whole life of the submarine without being refuelled. They were also bigger. This large reactor meant that Astute had to be a larger diameter boat than Trafalgar. The early idea of having a bulge around the reactor compartment didn't work out, and the new submarine ultimately became 40% larger than Trafalgar. A submarine is made up of dozens of separate systems, such as those which produce fresh air and fresh water and those that allow it to listen for adversary submarines through the ocean. It was intended that B2TC's systems would mostly be cut and pasted from Trafalgar. But some of Trafalgar's design elements stemmed from the 1950s and were clearly obsolete. Eventually, ten out of Astute's 13 major systems were either completely new or extensively modified.

But not only was Astute more complex than had been hoped, designing it was much harder than anticipated. As with the attempted Agile development of Universal Credit in the Department for Work and Pensions a decade later, introducing 3D-CAD into submarine design may have been the right thing to do, but the benefits didn't come quickly. The 3D-CAD system wasn't up to the challenge, and there were nowhere near enough CAD experienced designers for the job.

Meanwhile, the ownership structure of the Barrow shipyard changed yet again as British Aerospace merged with GEC Marconi to create BAE Systems. There was another period of instability and high staff turnover. Construction of HMS *Astute* eventually began in January 2001. But within a year, five years into the contract period, BAE Systems admitted that the boat was three years behind schedule. The first response from Whitehall was to bring in outsiders to work out how to bring the project back on schedule. The assumption that there are always remedies for a failing project, that those at the coalface are too stupid or unimaginative to see, is another attribute of the inverse square law. For Astute, retaining 2005 delivery was already a pipe dream. The reality was that the delivery capability of the shipyard was simply too undersized and inexperienced for the job.

BAE Systems, having inherited a contract with a maximum price, and a project with no end in sight, were pouring money into an apparently bottomless pit. Not even a company of BAE Systems scale could bear the unlimited risk of continuing on these terms. So, in 2003, six years into the contract, the MoD was dragged back to the negotiating table. In the renegotiation, most of the aggressive commercial approaches of the government's original delivery strategy were reversed. The ministry took back the risks that it thought it had transferred to the supplier and began to rebuild its capability to oversee the project in the shipyard. Ultimately, the MoD had to retreat completely from the strategy of contracting out the Design Authority. The maximum price condition was removed from the contract and instead the BAE Systems cost liability was capped so that it was the government that had to pay for the overruns. Embarrassingly, the MoD had to request support from the company which built nuclear submarines for the US Navy, which sent thirteen specialists over to Cumbria, supported by over a hundred Connecticut-based engineers, to try to bring the project under control.

The in-service date for the first boat moved back to 2008 and the government was forced once again to reduce its planned number of attack boats from 10 to 8.

Gradually the design problems were overcome, and some construction momentum was gained in the shipyard. Four years after the re-set, HMS *Astute* was finally launched into the Barrow dock in June 2007 in the presence of the Duchess of Cornwall and 10,000 spectators. But getting it into the water is only the start of the process of testing and commissioning a new nuclear submarine, and it was now a decade since the last time this had been done, and fully 17 years since a first-in-class boat had been at the same stage. Erosion of experience meant that, once again, everyone was learning on the job, and anyway most of the boat's systems were of new and more complex design. The boat wasn't ready to leave Barrow to begin the extensive sea-trials which a nuclear submarine must pass before becoming operational until November 2009. Predictably, the sea trials brought to light still more design and construction flaws and exposed the poor reliability of some of the new equipment. The boat made international news during its trials by becoming marooned on a sandbank off the Isle of Skye. HMS *Astute* didn't become fully operational until April 2013, 16 years after the contract was let. Without doubt it was the most expensive submarine ever built in the UK.

By now, not only had all of the Swiftsure class submarines been decommissioned, but two of the Trafalgar class boats had too. So rather than joining a fleet of 12 boats, as it would have if it had arrived on time in 2005, HMS *Astute* brought the complement of in-service boats up to just five. Just to maintain this strength, the remaining Trafalgar class boats had to operate well past their original design life.[6] In 2012, the situation was so dire that, for the first time, the Navy was unable to conduct the famous Perisher submarine command course to qualify new commanding officers.[7] There simply weren't enough boats.

The next 4 attack submarines, named *Artful, Ambush, Audacious* and *Anson*, followed HMS *Astute* into service over the next 11 years. They were commissioned at intervals about double those achieved by previous classes of nuclear submarine. The depleted attack submarine force, a consequence of the Astute project's failure, has been a disaster for the Royal Navy. The UK press reported in August 2024 that not a single Astute class operational voyage had been completed in the year.[8]

*

In retrospect, the recklessness of letting the nation's capacity to build nuclear submarines wither, abandoning the government's role as Design Authority, and trying to buy something as complex as a nuclear submarine at a competitive fixed price as if it were photocopy paper, is obvious. But at the time, the MoD and the centre of government were so far from the reality of submarine building as to be blind to the real challenge.

The solution is to recognise that the inverse square law works in reverse too. If you take two steps closer to the difficult business of actual delivery, and resist the temptation to assume that everyone involved is hopeless, then the challenges are four times easier to see. Anecdotes of politicians investing the time to do this are rare, but one was given to me about London Mayor Ken Livingstone during the development of the London Congestion Charging scheme, a novel and contentious project at the time. Reportedly, he rolled up his sleeves and got involved, understanding where policy had to be tweaked in order to make the project deliverable, and helping to break through barriers. But the Congestion Charging project was delivered within one term of the London mayoralty. Livingstone knew that he would be held accountable for whether it was completed on time, and whether it worked. But since the Astute project was conceived in the mid-1980s, there have been 25 Ministers for Defence Procurement. Few of them have had the time, let alone the incentive, to probe too deeply into the potential long-term consequences of their acts and omissions.

*

A few years ago, a high-profile advocate for more investment in railways in the UK told me that instead of approving HS2 as a one-off railway project, which would start from scratch and one day be complete, the government should instead have made a firm decision to spend, say, £4 billion every year on new railway capacity. Decisions about which specific railways to build could be taken over time. The important thing was to build a stable, learning enterprise – and then use it. I suspect he had his tongue fairly firmly in his cheek when he said it, but I do think that he was on to something.

Sponsoring, designing, building and commissioning major railways doesn't need skills and capabilities that are quite so unique as those you need for a nuclear submarine, but it isn't a game for amateurs either. Crossrail Ltd spent a decade learning how to do it, including finding out the hard way how difficult integrating a modern railway is. But rather than build on this learning, the country started again from scratch with HS2 Ltd. And now that this project has been up a steep learning curve, making plenty of mistakes of its own, it looks like its hard-won experience won't survive either. The next major rail project will no doubt require yet another arm's length delivery body and another blank sheet of paper. It isn't just the professional experience of individual project managers and engineers that is lost when this happens. It is also the rich warp and weft of institutional process and systems that will never be very effective when they are deployed for the first time. Perversely, the next arm's length delivery body may actively avoid recruiting people who have lived through, and learnt from, the HS2 experience so as to prevent the shiny new organisation being contaminated with failure.

It doesn't have to be like this. David Hughes, survivor of the Crossrail project, told me about what he had seen overseas.

> *I looked at the cost per kilometre of track electrification in other European countries – Germany in particular – compared to what we achieve in the UK. The difference is that they have a rolling programme, and they just keep churning out track electrification. They do it every year. It's the same client and the same supply chain and they know what they're doing.*

It is a sound bet that the later German electrification projects were quicker and cheaper than the first ones. In much larger and more complex projects, the value of continuity would be even greater.

This way of looking at long-term investments requires a move away from every project being treated as a one-off, and requires an appreciation of those project capabilities, both in government and the supply-chain, that can become national assets in their own right. It also requires longer-term planning and a sustained flow of investment if they are to become world class.

If we want to build fast combat jets, large nuclear power stations, small modular nuclear reactors, high-capacity railways or indeed nuclear submarines, then we have to stop thinking that it is easy. We need to nurture the public and private sector capabilities that are required to deliver them – and feed them with enough work to keep them fit. The alternative is repeatedly rebuilding capability that never gets to do anything for the second, third and fourth time. What you get, in other words, is projects like Astute.

8

NAIVETY: PRIVATISING SELLAFIELD

Civil servants don't pour concrete, weld metal or write computer code. Usually, they don't make detailed designs or painstaking delivery plans either. Overwhelmingly, this is done in the private sector by contractors and consultants. The question is not whether the private sector should be involved in the largest project challenges, but rather how to get them to do what you want them to do. This is not as easy as it sounds.

*

If ever there was a place that needs sustained nurturing of capability it is Sellafield. If you have ever looked out towards the Irish Sea from the top of England's highest hills on a rare clear day, then you will have seen it on the coastline. It is the place where Britain's most hazardous nuclear material is kept, including the world's largest stockpile of civil plutonium. The story of what happened at Sellafield between 2008 and 2016 brings together some of the tendencies we have already explored: the consequences of avoidable complexity, a wilful blindness to uncertainty, and a large dose of the inverse square law. But above all it is a story of naivety. With precious little evidence, the government became convinced that the local management of the site wasn't up to the job. With no evidence at all, they decided that private sector managers were bound to do a better job.

Much of what happens behind the razor wire around Sellafield is classified. But some of the challenges that the site faces are in the public domain. I can give you a sense of the mission by describing a single facility, one of dozens on the site. It is called the Magnox Swarf Storage Silo, MSSS, and it is one of the most hazardous places in Britain.[1]

Like the nation's nuclear submarines, MSSS is a child of the Cold War. The 1946 McMahon Act of Congress banned the US from exporting nuclear warheads. So if Britain was to develop its own nuclear deterrent, then the warheads would have to be made at home, and that needed plutonium. The UK's first production scale nuclear reactor was built at Sellafield on the site of an old munitions factory. You can find some grainy black and white newsreel film on YouTube of the plant being opened by the Queen in 1956. Known as a Magnox reactor, it was the world's first commercial nuclear power station, exporting electricity to the power grid. In fact, electricity was a by-product. Its primary role was to produce plutonium for the atomic weapons programme. But electricity wasn't the only by-product. When the fuel rods became depleted and were removed from the reactor, the material used to clad the fuel had to be stripped off. The used cladding, known as swarf, looked innocent enough, but the scientists operating the reactor knew it would be dangerously radioactive for hundreds of years. To make handling it more difficult, the swarf was made of magnesium, which meant that it ignited easily and needed to be kept underwater. The swarf reacted with the water to generate hydrogen, which is itself highly explosive. In the race to keep up with the Russians, the priority was the atomic weapons programme, not the disposal of waste, so a quick and dirty solution to the problem of storing the swarf was built in a hurry. It was nothing more than a large silo filled with water, into which the swarf, and any other waste that was proving inconvenient, could be dumped. Over the next three decades, as more Magnox reactors came on stream across the country, the MSSS silo was extended three times. But an indefinite number of silo extensions was clearly not the permanent answer and, as the Cold War came to an end, alternative storage solutions were found for fuel cladding. This only left the small matter of emptying the silos. In their haste, scientists and engineers had built the silos to be filled, not emptied, and now this Cold War legacy had to be addressed. It is hard to conceive the scale of MSSS without seeing it. The silo has 22 individual compartments, each large enough to hold six double-decker buses. Under the surface of the water, which has itself become a major hazard, there are 10,000m³ of waste. And there are no good records of what is in which compartment. Emptying MSSS is one of the nation's most hazardous nuclear challenges.

This is just one amongst dozens of examples of Sellafield's new mission: tackling the nation's nuclear legacy.

*

I first stood on the viewing platform overlooking MSSS in 2007, when I was still new to leading the Major Projects Directorate in the Office of Government Commerce. I had gone to the site to try to understand what the government department responsible for nuclear facilities, then called BERR, Business, Energy and Regulatory Reform, was planning for Sellafield. Their plan was not specific to MSSS, but involved management of decommissioning for the whole site, a job that will last well into the 22nd century. The BERR officials in Whitehall had tried to explain it to me, but I just couldn't understand the logic of what they were proposing. 'It's in the 2004 Energy Act', I was told, 'the decision is taken'. So I went to see for myself. But no-one I spoke to at Sellafield could really explain why the strategy would work either, and I left the site none-the-wiser. It is the greatest regret of my time in the Office of Government Commerce that I didn't make more of a fuss about what government wanted to do. I don't suppose it would have made any difference, but I wish I had made more noise. What I didn't realise at the time was that I wasn't alone in my scepticism. The following year, the National Audit Office concluded that the Department's plans were 'unlikely to encourage sites to deliver long-term value for money'.[2]

*

At the end of 2008, the management of Sellafield was out-sourced to Nuclear Management Partners, a consortium led by the US federal government contractor URS, for an anticipated contract period of 17 years. To understand why, you have to go back to the beginning of the decade. At that time, Sellafield was part of a UK government owned business called British Nuclear Fuels Ltd - BNFL. Unlike Crossrail Ltd, HS2 Ltd, and the other government companies described in this book, BNFL wasn't set up to deliver a government mission. It was a commercially driven enterprise, and its job was to make money for the Treasury. Although it was responsible for decommissioning, its core business was manufac-turing nuclear fuel, generating electricity from the fleet of Mag-nox reactors, and reprocessing spent fuel. Over the years, it had become a major international business, and in the 1990s it had been on an acquisition spree, purchasing, amongst other things, Westinghouse Electric Company, an American commercial nuclear power business. The government decided to monetise what looked like a successful business through some form of privatisation. But by the turn of the century, it was clear that the company's nuclear liabilities in the UK made the business unsaleable and, in any case, some of the company's foreign ventures were in quite a lot of trou-ble. In 2000, the company posted its largest ever loss. Government lost confidence in the commercial business and began to consider alternatives for dealing with the nuclear legacy at the company's UK sites, the largest of which by far was Sellafield. Privatisation was postponed.

Government's first problem at the legacy sites was that keeping the radioactive inventories, including the swarf in MSSS, safe and secure was costing billions every year. Sellafield alone had 10,000 employees and 1,000+ contractors. The second problem was that simply storing the nuclear waste in its current form was unsustain-able. The older facilities on the site were at or beyond their design life and they wouldn't last forever. The oldest portion of MSSS, for example, had begun to leak radioactive liquor to the ground in the 1970s, and although the leak had mysteriously stopped after a time, the only way to guarantee that it wouldn't start again was to empty the silos. Nobody knew how that could be done, but engineers were working on a series of projects to try to tackle the problem. Their idea was to build a series of machines which would operate as a massive version of the kind of lucky grabber that you pay a pound to use at an amusement arcade. These grabbers would weigh 400 tonnes, be over 6 metres tall, and take many years to design, build and install. Whatever they grabbed would be lowered into large boxes which would then be encapsulated for safety in a large new plant before being transported to new cathedral-sized storage facilities. Emptying the silos would take decades. All the facilities would have to be built in such a way as to prevent anybody ever being exposed to the radioactive hazard posed by the swarf. The very long-term strategy was to retrieve the boxes from Sellafield's stores and deposit them in a Geological Disposal Facility where the hazard would be put beyond reach. But it was anybody's guess how long that would take, so the waste was expected to remain at Sellafield for up to a century. Even then, once these facilities became redundant, they would themselves become nuclear waste and have to be disposed of. All of this project work would require billions of pounds' worth of new investments at the site. Sellafield was already spending around £300 million a year on new projects and that was bound to grow significantly. If this all sounds difficult, remember that MSSS is only one of many hazards that the site had to deal with.

The third problem was the one the Treasury worried most about. From an accounting point of view, the future cost of dealing with the nation's nuclear waste didn't only make BNFL unsaleable, it sat on the government's balance sheet as a liability – money the government will one day have to spend. And liabilities limit the amount of money the government can borrow to spend on other things the nation needs, like schools and hospitals. So reducing the nation's nuclear liability efficiently and cost-effectively was an imperative for the centre of government.

In 2002, faced with these two issues inside BNFL – a troubled international commercial business that was proving unsaleable, and a large nuclear liability at Sellafield and elsewhere that had to be reduced – government concluded that if BNFL had done a poor job of running its commercial business, then it must be doing a poor job of decommissioning. Its answer was an outsourcing competition. They knew that no private sector entity would take over accountability for the actual waste – a liability so huge that even Her Majesty's Treasury was worried about it – but perhaps they could find bidders for a contract to manage the site. Stronger private sector management, they thought, if provided with enough commercial incentive, was bound to bring momentum and innovation to the clean-up, making it faster and cheaper. The contractor would be paid if they met what the Department's 2002 White Paper described as, 'simple, objective and output-oriented goals and targets'.[3] It was the commercial naivety of this idea that I couldn't get my mind around in 2007.

Government's first step was to set up Sellafield as a separate company with its own board of directors. The new Sellafield Ltd was given a licence to operate the site by the Health and Safety Executive's Nuclear Installations Inspectorate.[4] The licence set out the company's responsibility for keeping Sellafield safe. But the company would also need a client in government, so the Department created an arm's length body, the Nuclear Decommissioning Authority, the NDA, to manage a contract between the government and Sellafield Ltd, and similar contracts with the site licence holders of the other legacy sites. This new structure was in place at Sellafield by 2005. The plan from there was to run a competition to procure a private sector company to take ownership of Sellafield Ltd for a set period. The new owner, to be called the Parent Body Organisation, or PBO, would put its own management team into the company to drive performance, and inject whatever technical, commercial and project management resources it needed to meet the targets in the contract, without breaching the conditions of the site licence. All the costs of running the site would be reimbursed to the company, including the cost of the people the PBO brought in, and a fee would be paid on top as progress was made against the targets and goals. The NDA would withhold fees if the company's performance was unsatisfactory. The bidders would make their money by taking dividends out of Sellafield Ltd.

The government's original idea had been to test this model on a low-level waste disposal site called Drigg, a few miles from Sellafield. Drigg is orders of magnitude simpler than Sellafield and this trial run might have provided an opportunity to learn about how the PBO model worked – or didn't work. But, in the NDA, belief in the strategy had become so strong that they decided to go ahead with the untested model for Sellafield without waiting to see how it turned out at Drigg. One veteran of the time remembers the ideological fervour as being like a cult. No one was allowed to voice scepticism about whether this commercial strategy would work.

So, in 2007, the Sellafield competition was launched and in 2008, Nuclear Management Partners became the Parent Body Organisation for Sellafield Ltd.

*

The first contributor to failure of the Sellafield privatisation was our old foe complexity. Government charged the NDA with the challenge of reducing the nation's nuclear liability. The NDA held contracts with Sellafield Ltd to operate the site with that objective. Sellafield Ltd was owned by a Parent Body Organisation and was licenced by an independent safety regulator. Sellafield Ltd let contracts with other private sector contractors to deliver the actual projects on the site. The PBO was incentivised to improve Sellafield's performance by meeting targets in the contracts between Sellafield Ltd and the NDA. This is a very simplified version of the government's plan. A full explanation would take a couple of hours at a whiteboard. All the players on the pitch were new, and no-one really knew exactly what everybody else's role was in practice.

But the problem of complexity was dwarfed by the second contributor – uncertainty. Sellafield, like all the other sites, had a plan for how the site was to be decommissioned. Called the Lifetime Plan, it laid out all the work that would be required over more than a century to make Sellafield into a nuclear-free site again. The bidders had all been given the Lifetime Plan and had bid to improve upon it through the duration of their ownership of the site. To realise how naive this idea was, I want you to conduct a quick thought experiment. Imagine that you ran a painting and decorating firm and were asked to bid to redecorate a room. The householder had a plan for how long it would take – stripping the wallpaper, painting the ceiling and skirting boards, and hanging new paper. But when you ask to see the room, you are not allowed to enter it. The door is boarded up and all the windows are blacked out. Then you find out that the householder has never been in the room either, and has no idea about the state of the decoration, whether there's any damp, or even whether the floor is solid enough to work on. You might give them a quote, but you would hedge it with all kinds of assumptions and make sure that they were taking all the risk about the actual condition of the room. MSSS is such a room. And Sellafield has a whole mansion of rooms that no one can enter. So the Lifetime Plan may have been a necessary tool for guessing the nuclear liability to hold on government's balance sheet, but as a plan of how much work was actually involved, it was a work of fiction.

The fundamental problem was that the outcomes that the government wanted – and was prepared to pay for – were very, very, long term. But the incentives on the PBO had to be short term. The PBO and the NDA agreed an annual plan, with milestones and performance indicators, but there was always a good reason why the plan changed, and every change let the PBO off the hook. Sometimes the changes were due to the intrinsic uncertainty of the work, sometimes they were imposed by the safety regulator, and sometimes they were required by the NDA itself. Often this was due to the way government required the NDA to manage its business. As well as managing the nuclear legacy, the NDA was making money from the last two operational Magnox power-stations in the country, and a large nuclear fuel reprocessing business inherited from BNFL. These were profitable businesses, and the income from them was included in the budget the NDA was given by government. But although they were profitable, they were also volatile. Sometimes the power-stations and the reprocessing plants came off-line unexpectedly. When this happened the NDA had to cut how much it could spend that year, and that would mean less money for decommissioning at the nuclear sites. Once again, the PBO had an excuse for under-delivering, and the NDA's oversight was focussed not on the progress with decommissioning, but with balancing its books by the end of the year.

A final example will be enough to show why the commercial model was never going to work. The PBO was incentivised to deliver efficiencies. Fair enough. If you do it cheaper then you get a portion of the savings. But the efficiencies were measured against budgets, so if the PBO could get a large budget for a task, and then beat it, they made money. It's true that the NDA had to agree the budget, but how could they challenge the cost for dealing with what was in the boarded-up room? They couldn't scrutinise the costs that went into the estimates that went into the budget, so all they could do was scrutinise the *process* that was used to derive them. This was a game the PBO knew it could win. The innovation that the private sector brought was not so much into how to decommission the site, but how to game the contract.

Four years into the contract, the National Audit Office reported that, in 2011, Nuclear Management Partners had been paid fees of £54 million with little evidence of performance improvement.[5] The 14 major projects being run by Sellafield Ltd were plagued by delays and extra costs. When the auditors returned in 2015, the project performance was even worse. And every time the PBO turned over a stone on the site, they claimed that the scale of their task had gone up. The cost of running the site grew and grew – as did the nuclear liability. This was the exact opposite of what government had naively hoped would happen.

The PBO executives in charge of Sellafield did themselves no favours in terms of public opinion. In the first three years of the contract, they were reported to have awarded themselves more than £6 million in bonuses.[6] And the nation's press loved the story that they had been required to repay thousands of pounds in expenses after an audit uncovered travel junkets to the US Masters golf tournament, gourmet dinners in France, and a £714 taxi bill for transporting a senior manager's cat.

In January 2015, the NDA terminated the PBO contract, and in April 2016, Sellafield Ltd came back into public ownership. By 2023, all of the other sites had followed. The whole experiment had failed. I have heard the period of private ownership described as Sellafield's lost decade.

*

This whole sorry story stems from one of the most common and naive misconceptions about public sector projects – the myth that the private sector is bound to do a better job than the public sector.

In the case of Sellafield, the government, and the Nuclear Decommissioning Authority, were both convinced that more commercial management would lead to better decision making, more efficiency and greater innovation. In fact, it led to more commercial focus on how to maximise the profit of the Parent Body Organisation.

Sellafield and the other nuclear sites are not the only example of the 'private sector good, public sector bad' mantra. In the 1990s, the Atomic Weapons Establishment, the part of the MoD which makes nuclear warheads, was given over to the private sector before being brought back into public ownership due to poor management, safety problems and several large project failures. The Royal Dockyards at Rosyth and Devonport were privatised too, and so far remain in the private sector. And in 2012, the Ministry of Defence tried to outsource management of its entire procurement and project management organisation. The Defence think-tank RUSI commented,

> The proposal ... appears to rest on an argument that, because the government is not very good at negotiating and managing contracts with the private sector, it is going to negotiate an even bigger contract with a private sector entity to undertake the entire task on its behalf.[7]

Thankfully for the sake of the nation's defence, the competition fell apart when all but one bidder backed out. What these examples all have in common is that the organisations in question exist only to fulfil a complex and highly uncertain governmental objective – safely storing nuclear waste, manufacturing nuclear warheads, servicing Royal Navy ships and submarines, procuring defence equipment. They are not businesses, like British Telecom or British Gas. They are all undertaking the inherently governmental activity of being the public sector client. This is what makes putting them in private sector hands so problematic. How do you incentivise a commercial entity to deliver something so uncertain? As at Sellafield, most of the apparent risk transfer will prove to be an illusion. The consequences of poor performance are always borne by the government.

*

Privatising and outsourcing aren't the only way to try to bring private sector disciplines to bear on large public sector project delivery challenges. Some of the others have been somewhat more successful. The first alternative is to try to mimic private sector ownership and management, but without the profit motive that drove such perverse behaviours at Sellafield. This is how you end up with arm's length bodies like Crossrail Ltd and the Restoration and Renewal Delivery Authority. They look a bit like a normal company, led by executives and non-executives with a mix of private and public sector experience, and operate, theoretically, under some kind of contract with their government sponsors. It is an attempt to get the best of both worlds. The record, to say the least, is mixed.

The next approach is to create some kind of alliance or partnership between the public sector and the private sector deliverers. The idea is to keep the public sector firmly at the table, while binding the private sector companies into commonly owned plans and goals. Something like this is now being tried for the largest projects at Sellafield. The partners are not running the site, but they do run the projects. If (and it is a big if), the client really knows what they want, and the leaders can navigate their different incentives, this idea might work.

Finally, you can get the private sector to put its money where its mouth is. There was a slew of such projects under the last Labour government under the label of PFI, the Private Finance Initiative. Here, the finance markets would provide the capital to a consortium which delivered the project. The investors took their returns in fees paid by the government through the life of the asset. The original objectives of PFI were financial – keeping the assets off the government's balance sheet and paying for them on the never-never rather than out of today's budgets. But there was a spin off benefit. If the risk could genuinely be passed to the investors, they brought private sector rigour to bear to make sure the project delivered on time and on budget. It worked well when the scope of the project was firmly nailed down and didn't change. It is too early to be sure at the time of writing, but it looks as though this has worked for Transport for London's £1.2 billion Silvertown Tunnel project, which will provide the first new road crossing east of Tower Bridge for over 30 years. The forecast is that it will open ahead of schedule. The project consortium's job has been to make money for their owners by beating the plan. Transport for London's job has been to keep out of their way and resist the temptation to tweak the scope.

But PFI only has a chance of working when the scope is firm, and the market is genuinely prepared to take the delivery risk. And there isn't a single project in this book for which the market would be prepared to do that. Indeed, this is the whole justification for the government taking on huge projects in the first place. Government has to run the projects which are too risky for the market. And that is a category into which managing Sellafield definitely fits.

9

ARROGANCE: THE NHS
NATIONAL PROGRAMME

Before turning to the more positive question of what we can do about it, I have one last story of failure. Some of its elements will be beginning to sound familiar by now. It starts with untrammelled wishful thinking about what could be achieved, married to a complete lack of imagination about what might go wrong. Without the levers to compel compliance, this project attempted to impose strict standardisation on a hugely complex delivery environment. Messianic conviction amongst its leaders overrode informed objections and they condemned all critics as vested interests or forces of reaction. They convinced themselves that their supply chain could work miracles at unprecedented pace, while accepting immense levels of risk. And when the inevitable problems overtook the project, they persisted with it for years.[1]

*

In February 2002, Prime Minister Tony Blair hosted a seminar in Downing Street. He was convinced that the National Health Service in England could be transformed with the help of better IT. It was said that he had been enthused about the subject after a discussion with Microsoft CEO Bill Gates. Blair himself was there for less than an hour, but those present, including the Department of Health ministerial team of Alan Milburn and Lord Hunt, senior executives from NHS England, and several senior representatives of the IT industry, came away convinced that a step-change in the use of computers could make enough of a difference to NHS performance that Labour would be rewarded by voters at the next election. Milburn and the NHS committed to present the Prime Minister with a national implementation plan by the end of May. It would set a timetable for hospitals and GPs to benefit from a network of new systems. Implementation of new IT would start within a year.[2]

This Downing Street meeting has gone down in history as a classic example of Blair's 'sofa-cabinet' style of governing – blue-sky thinking leading to informal and poorly considered decisions. The charge is not entirely fair. The role that IT would have to play in modernising the NHS was already firmly established. A year earlier, Chancellor Gordon Brown had commissioned banker Derek Wanless to investigate what was required to turn the NHS in England into a service which provided safer, higher quality treatment. Amongst other findings, Wanless was scathing about the NHS's use of IT. He concluded that, 'A major programme will be required to establish the infrastructure and to ensure that common standards are established. Central standards must be set and rigorously applied.' He seemed to be advocating a mandated, top-down implementation of new IT systems, and that is exactly what, following the Downing Street meeting, the Government embarked upon.[3]

The prospectus for a massive IT Project for Health, to be known as the National Programme, was published in June.[4] It promised greater central control and ruthless standardisation. The scope of the programme was rather vague but would include new infrastructure and a number of services including a national booking service, a national prescriptions service, and a national health records service which would be accessible round the clock from anywhere in the country. Shorn of draft sections on the risks involved, what was published was not a long document.[5] The important thing was to get going. By September, the National Programme was launched, and an external expert had been hired to run it. His name was Richard Granger, a consultant from Deloitte. He had no background in health, but he did have a reputation for hard-nosed delivery, most recently deployed in the successful London Congestion Charging scheme. On appointment, he was reputed to be the country's highest paid civil servant.

Granger quickly developed a plan for procuring the new systems. To counter the risk of lashing the NHS to a single IT provider, Granger decided to divide the country into five regions and procure a monopoly service into each one. As with the Astute Submarine project a decade earlier, the idea was to generate an intense competition and to load the supply chain up with as much risk as possible. In the National Programme, suppliers would be paid nothing until they delivered working services. And anyone not performing would have their region taken from them and redistributed to the other suppliers. Granger told the media that if you are using huskies to pull you to the pole, then

> *when one of the dogs goes lame, and begins to slow the others down, they are shot. They are then chopped up and fed to the other dogs. The survivors work harder, not only because they've had a meal, but also because they have seen what will happen should they themselves go lame.*[6]

The survival of the fittest was bound to work for large IT companies too. You might think that conditions like this would scare off any potential bidders, but if you are in the business of selling IT services to government, then these potential contracts are too big to ignore. By the end of 2003, the five regional contracts had been let to four providers: BT, Accenture, Fujitsu and an American company, CSC, which won two regions. Although there were four service providers, they had between them only two developers for the most important of the new software solutions. These electronic patient record systems would allow information to be exchanged seamlessly between healthcare professionals, managers and patients. BT and Fujitsu selected a US company, IDX, and Accenture and CSC chose the UK firm, iSoft. The ten-year contracts had a total value of £6.2 billion.[7]

Granger's commercially aggressive approach won him plenty of fans in the centre of government. When I arrived in Whitehall in 2007, he was a model for the kind of hard-nosed leader that government projects needed. The Treasury selected him as one of the first appointees to the new Major Projects Review Group. The BBC included him in a Radio 4 documentary dedicated to 'Britain's Modern Brunels'. The National Audit Office was impressed too. In their first review of the programme, in 2006, they lauded the speed of the procurement, and the principle of payment by results.[8]

The project was intended to revolutionise the way healthcare was provided, bringing huge benefits for health professionals and their patients. But the input from clinicians into what the new systems would have to do was superficial to say the least. A director of the NHS Information Authority told the Public Accounts Committee two years later that the consultation process amounted to 'asking some clinicians to comment on hundreds of pages of text in systems-speak in the space of a few weeks'.[9] Just as happened in the Universal Credit project a decade later, all the complexities emerged after the work began. But at least with Universal Credit the ultimate objective of the new systems was reasonably clear. The Chair of the National Clinical Advisory Board told the same Public Accounts Committee that the NHS National Programme

> *was like being in a juggernaut lorry going up the M1 and it did not really matter where you went as long as you arrived somewhere on time... To be honest, I do not think the people selling it knew what we needed.*

Perhaps in recognition of the lack of clinical understanding in the project, Professor Aidon Halligan, the deputy Chief Medical Officer, was appointed to work alongside Granger as joint head of the project in the spring of 2004. But it was too late to influence the contracts which had already been signed. These health experts found escape routes from the project, but none of them went public. The director of the NHS Information Authority was made redundant, the Chair of the National Clinical Advisory Board was asked to resign, and Professor Halligan quit his role in the project after six months, although he stayed on as deputy Chief Medical Officer.

Procured in a hurry, and without sufficient involvement from NHS professionals, neither of the electronic patient record system developers, IDX or iSoft, were able to get to grips with the complexities of healthcare provision in the NHS. The extremely aggressive commercial approach imposed by Granger produced predictably miserable results. Neither Accenture nor CSC could get the iSoft package working despite spending large amounts of money. Accenture made a $450 million provision in their global accounts to cover losses made on the National Programme and began to talk about cutting their losses and pulling out of the project altogether.[10] In response, Granger threatened them with a huge penalty of half of the contract value. But when Accenture finally did walk away, their threatened counterclaim against the National Programme meant that they paid only £63 million in penalties.[11] CSC, also in trouble with the iSoft solution, but not yet ready to write-down their investments, was faced with a double or quits decision. Still hoping for success, they agreed to take on Accenture's region as well as their own. Fujitsu, who had opted for the IDX solution, were struggling too. Granger allowed them to drop IDX and move to a different American provider, Cerner. As BT struggled on with the IDX solution, Granger threatened then with the husky solution – 'We will very soon get to the point where they will either come good with what they've got, or they will get a bullet in the head' – before letting BT swap to the Cerner solution too.[12]

A large part of the problem was underappreciation of the fundamental differences between how healthcare is provided on different sides of the Atlantic. In the United States, the health system is administered so as to bill insurers or patients for every intervention. This isn't how UK hospitals work. And no-one in the US health system has to administer patient waiting lists – a matter of huge importance in the NHS. Fujitsu progress was sufficiently poor that their contract was terminated in 2008, and the work handed over to BT. There were now only two regional suppliers and two electronic patient record system developers, and none of them were making acceptable progress.

Parts of the clinical community were now in open revolt. Some were beginning to question what the whole programme was really all for.[13] Having spent years blaming the IT suppliers, Granger now turned his fire on the NHS itself. If there was a problem, it was not with the IT, but with the clinicians. 'If some of my colleagues do not think sufficiently through as to what was wanted then it's a specification error'.[14] One health professional posted his disgust: 'Now and then I check myself from hatred of what Richard Granger stands for and has done to NHS IT, and then the sheer arrogance and ignorance of his public statements brings me back.'[15]

It was evident by 2007 that centrally implemented system deployments were not achieving the project's objectives. But the NHS was still wedded to the need for enforced commonality. So NHS Chief Executive David Nicholson announced that from this point on the project would retain the mandated regional monopoly system suppliers, but that deployment would be devolved to the ten Strategic Health Authorities. The apparently confused thinking behind this decision was mirrored in the name given to the change. It was called the 'National Programme Local Ownership Plan', NLOP. It was quickly characterised as 'No Longer Our Problem'.[16]

Although the project limped on for another three years, 2008 was the year in which hope seems to have left the project team. Richard Granger exited quietly at the beginning of the year. Accenture and Fujitsu were gone. BT and CSC were facing huge losses. Neither of the solution providers was delivering software that was up to the job. Virtually nothing was being deployed into NHS hospitals. The Trusts which could do so kept their heads down to wait the project out. The problems, always an open secret in the NHS, were now making national news. *The Guardian* reported that where new systems were being deployed, lack of patient data was causing delays in Accident and Emergency, cancer treatment and planned operations. Patients were exposed to the risk of infection while records were being updated manually, and in one Trust complaints from the public about their service tripled.[17] In what could have been the final nail in the coffin, the NAO reported that the programme had largely failed to deliver on its central objective.

Ministers, however, were still in denial, at least in public. As late as the end of 2009, Health Secretary Andy Burnham was defending the programme in the House of Commons. 'We have no intention whatsoever of cancelling the programme overall, not least because it is already making the NHS safer, more efficient and more convenient for patients.'[18] But in the Treasury, Chancellor Alistair Darling was already taking money from the project's budget.

*

Eventually, after the 2010 general election, the Coalition Government killed off the NHS National Programme. In a mealy-mouthed press-release, the Department of Health announced that 'a centralised, national approach is no longer required, and that a more locally-led plural system of procurement should operate, whilst continuing with national applications already procured'. The newly appointed Health Minister, Simon Burns, was only marginally less oblique. 'Improving IT is essential to delivering a patient-centred NHS. But the nationally imposed system is neither necessary nor appropriate to deliver this. We will allow hospitals to use and develop the IT they already have....'[19]

To be fair to the hundreds of professionals in the National Programme over the years, there were some strands of the project that were completed and eventually gained an enduring place in the NHS. These included 'Choose and Book', which allowed patients to select a hospital outpatient appointment from a range of options while sitting with their GP, and 'National Spine', a messaging service which allowed authorised users to access a high-level summary of patient records. But the electronic patient record systems at the heart of the programme were a complete failure, which cost years of potential improvement across the NHS. Overall, the National Programme had been a disaster.

The project is a tragic case-study of how not to manage IT enabled change. You start with blindly ambitious but inexact requirements and proceed through commercially naive contracts with impossible timeframes. The results are entirely predictable. The National Programme was swamped by technical and delivery complexity. The systems' end-users were kept as far away from involvement as possible. Lengthening timelines were met by refusal to acknowledge reality and the project ploughed on until it finally suffered the huskies' fate that Granger had predicted for some of the IT companies.

*

The years lost during the failed NHS National Programme have seriously retarded the digital transformation of health provision in England. Twenty-two years after the programme was conceived, a new Health Secretary, Wes Streeting, asked surgeon, academic and peer Lord Darzi to diagnose the ills of the NHS. Amongst many other criticisms Darzi took aim at the NHS's failure to embrace digital technologies.

> *The NHS remains in the foothills of digital transformation.... The NHS, in common with most health systems, continues to struggle to fully realise the benefits of information technology. It always seems to add to the workload of clinicians rather than releasing more time to care by simplifying the inevitable administrative tasks that arise. The extraordinary richness of NHS datasets is largely untapped either in clinical care, service planning, or research.*[20]

10

FASTER, HIGHER, STRONGER:
THE OLYMPICS PROJECTS

The rest of this book is devoted to what is going wrong at a systemic level, and what has to change so that we can do better. But first I want to talk about the main exception to this dismal record: the programme rightly celebrated for delivering all the construction projects required for the 2012 London Olympics. This is not only to relieve the gloom, but also because, of all the lessons learnt from the Olympics, the one which I hear most often is just plain wrong.

*

Imagine the scene inside the Whitehall offices of a major government project. The table is scattered with papers showing bar charts, dashboards, progress reports and risk registers. Most of the traffic lights are Red. A master-schedule, which everyone seemed to believe in a few years ago, is still on the wall. But the float has eroded to almost nothing. Every month seems to bring more bad news. Delivery managers presenting their progress reports are careful to say that the timeline can still be met, 'but we will have to roll a lot of sixes' – as though the laws of probability might have been suspended. In public, the project end-date has not moved. But the National Audit Office's fieldwork is nearly complete and everyone round the table knows what their report is going to say. A date for a Public Accounts Committee hearing is in the diary.

I have been in rooms like this on many projects. At some point someone will say, 'If only we'd had a completely immovable end-date like the Olympics. Nothing was allowed to stand in the way. If everyone on our project had that level of commitment, then we wouldn't be in this mess.' The reason the Olympic projects were successful, in this version of history, is that everybody knew that the opening ceremony was going to happen on 27th July 2012, come what may. There was no alternative, and nowhere to hide. Time and again I have heard this prescription presented as the main learning from the 2012 Olympics programme. It stems from the trauma of feeling accountable for a schedule that you know in your heart you will not deliver. You have been let down. If only every person, from the minister on the fifth floor to the welder in the factory, had known there was no choice...

When you feel impotent in the face of the forces that beset huge projects, this is a seductive thought. The problem is that it is not true. It is the same wishful thinking that led the Crossrail project to delude itself that the railway would be ready in 2018 because 'the Queen is booked!'.

Just to be clear, it certainly helps to have the rock-solid political commitment that the Olympics programme enjoyed. When I first met David Higgins, the Chief Executive of the Olympic Delivery Authority, in his 24th floor Canary Wharf office, he opened his desk draw and waved a laminated copy of the letter Prime Minister Blair and Chancellor Brown had written to the International Olympic Committee. It was as close as you can get to a blank cheque. In short, it underwrote the UK Government's investment in the Games and committed to doing whatever it took to be successful. If you are delivering a project, this is not unhelpful. And no doubt some of the stadium projects would indeed have overrun if there had been no fixed date for the opening ceremony. But the fixed end-date isn't the over-riding explanation for the Olympics triumph. There are reasons why the Olympic projects were successful – but having a non-negotiable end-date is not particularly high on the list.

*

After a failed attempt by Birmingham and two by Manchester, Tessa Jowell, then Secretary of State for Culture, Media and Sport, had got the message that London was the only city with a realistic chance of bringing the Games to Britain. The formal selection process to host the Games of the XXX Olympiad took place in 2005 from a short-list of five cities: London, Madrid, Moscow, New York and Paris. Paris was the longstanding favourite, but strikes and civil disruption during International Olympic Committee visits seemed to have dented their chances. In a ceremony in Singapore in July, the London bid, led by Sebastian Coe and the London Mayor Ken Livingstone, with star quality provided by David Beckham and Prince William, narrowly beat the French to win the chance to host. Tony Blair, who was hosting a G8 meeting at Gleneagles at the time, was jubilant. 'It's not often in this job that you punch the air and do a little jig and embrace the person next to you.'

Winning the bid took almost everybody by surprise. It certainly sent shockwaves through the Treasury, who had not paid much attention to the cost estimates on the assumption that Britain would again fail to win. Jowell's Department of Culture Media and Sport seemed an unlikely home for the nation's most high-profile project. When the bid for the Games was won, the site of the future Olympic Park, which would house not only a new major stadium and numerous smaller venues, but also accommodation for over 17,000 athletes, was a neglected corner of East London, heavily contaminated from previous industrial use and with poor transport links. DCMS was going to have to coordinate site reclamation, stadium construction, a major housing development, and significant new transport infrastructure, not to mention policing and security projects. Without any direct political control, they would have to spearhead projects from across numerous central government departments, Ken Livingstone's Greater London Authority and many of London's Boroughs. It was to be the largest single cross-government effort in Britain's peacetime history. No wonder there were sceptics about whether one of the smallest departments in Whitehall would be able to pull it off.

Jowell set up a new unit, the Government Olympic Executive, to coordinate across government, to sponsor the development of the Olympic Park, and to supervise the public sector budget. Then, in the first large deployment of the arm's length delivery organisation model subsequently used on HS2, Crossrail, and the Restoration and Renewal project, she steered a bill through Parliament to establish the Olympic Delivery Authority to take charge of the site preparation and construction of the venues and infrastructure. The ODA had a rough start. Its Chair, Jack Lemley, was a tough American engineer who had built his UK reputation by, reportedly, rescuing the Channel Tunnel project. But within a year he resigned, blaming political infighting and the unwillingness of government to face up to reality.[1] The real problem was the budget. Back in the bidding phase, with institutional confidence in winning low, and little Treasury scrutiny, the budget had been set at around £4 billion, 80% of which would come from Government. But this had underestimated the cost of remediating the site, hadn't included provision for policing and security, included virtually nothing for the cost of programme management and, amazingly, had ignored the need for the project to pay VAT on its spending. It had also made an unrealistically aggressive assumption about how much funding could be accessed from private sources. Finally, there was no contingency at all for the many things that would inevitably have to be dealt with over seven years of major project delivery. Getting approval for a new bottom-up budget, in March 2007, no doubt required considerable flourishing of the Blair/Brown letter to the IOC. The new cost was a huge £9.3 billion, nearly 30% of which was contingency.

From this point onwards, the Olympics programme is overwhelmingly a story of success. This isn't to say that the projects didn't suffer from the usual stresses and strains of project management. But the reclamation of a desolate piece of East London was a major achievement. The park, with its stadium, velodrome, and aquatic centre, not to mention large utilities and services projects, were all completed in time. An expansion of the London Overground rail network and upgrades to the Docklands Light Railway got finished. The largest bump in the road was the failure to obtain private finance to fund the athlete's village in the wake of the 2008 financial crash. The government had to fund the village with public money and sell it off after the Games. The last crisis happened when G4S, contracted to provide thousands of security staff, admitted two weeks before the opening ceremony that it had not recruited enough people. Thousands of members of the armed forces rode to the rescue.

*

Why was the programme for the Olympic Games so successful, if it wasn't as simple as having a fixed end-date? Every major endeavour needs some good fortune, but it wasn't just luck. Neither was it simply the law of averages – 'if you do enough multi-billion-pound projects then one day one of them will succeed!'. Before getting to the systemic reasons for the achievement, you have to start with the individual leaders who led the delivery – from Tessa Jowell, who remained the Government's champion of the Games up until the 2010 election despite successive ministerial demotions, to Jonathan Stephens, the Permanent Secretary of DCMS, who formed a tightly knit community of leaders with a shared intent, to David Higgins and John Armitt, who led the Olympic Delivery Authority through most of the project delivery phase. Collectively, they navigated elections which replaced one awkward Prime Minister/Mayor relationship, between Gordon Brown and Ken Livingstone, with another between David Cameron and Boris Johnson. They embraced a culture of openness to reality. They faced problems quickly and head-on, including acknowledging an inadequate budget early and taking the pain of reauthorisation with adequate contingency. The ODA's 24th floor perch overlooking the Olympic Park symbolised the short reporting lines. They were rarely in denial about the realities of delivery. Most importantly, the governance worked. Decision making was swift and effective.

But beyond the people, there are subtler characteristics of the Olympics programme that greatly increased the chances of success. They provide pointers to a better way for other huge government projects. In summary, the programme was clear-eyed about its ambition, it had enough contingency, its approach was as straightforward as possible, and it always had some room for manoeuvre.

There is a reason why the IOC award the Games seven years in advance. They know from experience that this is a doable duration within which to deliver the required investments. In other words, Beijing, Athens and Sydney each provided a meaningful reference class of similar endeavours. Seven years is not so long that cities can fudge and stall, and it is not so short that the projects required become undeliverable. Of course, not every Olympics is the same. The regeneration of a huge brown-field site in East London was a particular challenge. And the UK government didn't have the same autocratic freedoms that the Chinese state used to prepare for the 2008 Games in Beijing. But still, the schedule for 2012 preparation wasn't plucked out of the air or derived from a piece of optimistic clean-sheet-of-paper planning. The comparators gave very good reason to believe that it was doable. The schedule had, from the beginning, plenty of well-judged float. There was room for some things to go wrong. And unlike Crossrail or the smart metering infrastructure, a lot of delivery risk was retired early, in the planning and design phases. It was not all stacked up at the end in a massive system integration challenge.

Next, the Olympics programme was not a single project, but many. And while they all had to be complete by the time the Games started, they were, as projects, largely independent. When the private funding dried up for the Olympic Village, for example, the delay to that project did not infect everything else. So the overall challenge was broken down into manageable chunks. The chunks were significant projects in their own rights, but not highly inter-dependent multi-billion-pound behemoths. This reduced the complexity of the whole endeavour.

Finally, unlike many huge projects, despite the schedule being non-negotiable and the cost capped, there were scope levers to pull if things started to go wrong. If the cost of your railway project is unexpectedly inflated, you can't decide not to build the last few miles. If your submarine project is running late, you can't correct that by deciding not to bother with the sonar system. But with the Olympics projects, there were, until quite late in the programme life, options to de-scope in a way which might arguably impact on the legacy benefits, but which would not threaten the overall success of the Games. To take a single example, when money got tight, the intention to build a second 6,000 seat arena next to the

O2 in North Greenwich was scrapped and its events were moved to Wembley Arena.

So, without taking anything away from those who have been rightly garlanded for their achievement, the Olympics programme succeeded because it was doable from the beginning, with adequate contingency, it was broken down into discrete manageable chunks, and the scope was adjustable to cope with the inevitable problems that might arise.

A survivor of one of the failed projects in this book told me that 'the Olympics is a false god'. I think he meant that the Olympics programme wasn't as hard to deliver as his project – and he may have been right. But he thought that the lessons therefore didn't apply to him – and in this he was completely wrong. The Olympics programme had a high likelihood of success because it was set up to be achievable from the start. And, with the right commitment and leadership, it was achieved. Tony Meggs, the ex-Chief Executive of the Infrastructure and Projects Authority, and Chair of Crossrail, summed it up for me like this. 'Real performance comes from having a joint endeavour, where everybody feels both challenged and capable. It's realistic, it's achievable, and it has got some room for error in it.'

11

THE BUSINESS CASE FALLACY

Government has a process for developing projects. In principle, it is pretty straightforward. Three phases lead up to three decisions. Firstly, does the project make sense strategically? Second, when all the options have been considered, has the right one been chosen? And finally, once the project is fully developed, is it still right to go ahead?

Imagine that you work in National Highways, the organisation that looks after England's major road network. Let's say that amongst all the big traffic problems across England, the one that's reached the top of the pile is a serious bottleneck at a village called Hindhead on the A3 which runs from London to the Hampshire coast. It's quite an important road. The traffic backlogs frustrate drivers and residents, shatter the peace of a beautiful part of the North Downs, and throttle economic development in an area which could really do with more wealth creation. You decide that this is a problem that has to be solved. At this early stage, you should have an open mind about the scope of a project. Perhaps the right answer is a bypass, or maybe a tunnel. The Department for Transport might want to consider some way of incentivising traffic off the road onto the railway instead. But you should be able to explain why a project is the right answer and have very early views on how the problem could be solved, how long it might take and how much it might cost.

You write all this down in something called the 'Strategic Outline Business Case'. If you can convince the Department for Transport and get support from the Roads Minister, then you begin to explore the options for what the precise scope of the project might be. Your economic analysis concludes that the best ratio of benefits to costs is a tunnel that will make the road into a 70-mph dual-carriageway all the way from the outskirts of London to the coastal conurbation. You make very rough estimates of the cost and schedule, hopefully with some realism built into them, and you think that the project is affordable in the context of all the other demands on the roads budget. You begin to think about options for how to procure the design and construction and what kind of project team you will need to manage the project. But before you start a procurement process, you put the whole package together in an 'Outline Business Case' and get departmental and ministerial sign-off on your chosen option. Depending on the cost, you might need to convince the Treasury too. At this point, the amount you are spending ramps up as you set up a sizeable project team to pursue the planning consents and environmental assessments, as well as buying any land you require. When you're ready, you will go to market for detailed design and construction. Eventually, you have a project that is ready to proceed, and a contract ready to sign. Fingers crossed that your latest cost and time estimates are inside those signed off in the Outline Business Case. You bring this all together in a Final Business Case for presentation to the Transport Secretary and the Chief Secretary to the Treasury. If they still agree, then you have the green light to sign the contract and get going. A few years later, your tunnel is built, and the road can open. The bottleneck is gone. The people of Hindhead are delighted with their new peace and quiet, traffic moves to and fro between the coast and the capital. And visitors can enjoy the Devil's Punchbowl without the background noise of the A3. Happy Days.

This is the life of a public sector project professional. I have made it sound simple. In fact, it is extremely challenging. In the case of the Hindhead tunnel, just getting into the Government's strategic road programme took quarter of a century. Getting the final green light took six years more, and the road was opened five years later. In a project like this, there will be few nice surprises along the way and plenty of unpleasant ones. Technical issues are probably the least of the project manager's problems. There will be complex planning issues, public enquiries, hostile pressure groups, press scepticism, wavering political support and procurement legalities to negotiate, to name only a few. Hats off to everyone who manages to pull off a project like this. Just ask anyone who has been involved in what, on the surface, looks like a very similar project trying to tunnel past Stonehenge on the A303. That project has been on the drawing board since the mid-1990s. At the time of the 2024 general election, after many false-starts, the fully developed scheme seemed to be nearing the end of its convoluted legal battles against objectors, only for Chancellor Rachel Reeves to announced that the incoming Labour Government was cancelling the project, apparently permanently.

*

This three-stage process of developing a project; agreeing the strategy in a Strategic Outline Business Case, approving going to market through an Outline Business Case, and then authorising contract award in a Final Business Case, will be familiar to anyone who runs large projects in the private sector. The terminology will be different, the bureaucracy will be simpler, but essentially, this is how a project is run. Decision one – is it a good idea? Decision two – is this the right option for doing it? Decision three – now we know what it will cost and how long it will take, are we ok to get going? At the point of decision three, to take our road project example, the Government has essentially struck a deal with National Highways. 'We will give you this amount of money, and you will give us a road on time and on budget. Let us know when the Secretary of State can come and cut the ribbon.' Conceptually this can work quite well, whether we are talking about a road, a weapons system, or an IT project.

But what if we are talking not about a challenging road project, but digitising the last great analogue industry in the country? Or re-inventing the way a 70-year-old benefits system works? Or rewiring the largest bureaucracy in Europe, where every health trust has its own decision-making powers? Or completing the largest infrastructure project in the history of the country? Is it sensible to think of one of these monsters as a simple deal between a department and a delivery body, as if it were the project for the Hindhead Tunnel? Can we expect either side of this transaction to keep their word? Can a minister make a deal that will last for two or three election cycles, when the political consensus behind the project is flaky and insecure? Can the deliverer really predict how long something will take when it has never been done before? The largest government projects exist in an environment that is inherently random, chaotic and unpredictable. The world turns, governments fall, wars start, society changes, technologies emerge and die. The unthinkable becomes real and the certain becomes impossible. Starting a project like this is like starting a war. You can wargame outcomes. You can plan *for* it, but you can't plan it.

Our human nature, and the bureaucracies we create, struggle to accept just how radically uncertain the world around us is. We cope by creating a false sense of certainty. And that is exactly what we are doing when we apply the disciplines of project management to endeavours as uncertain as those in this book. Tony Meggs, who led the Infrastructure and Project Authority through most of the turbulent 2010s, describes it like this.

> *It is part of the human psyche to create a world in which you feel you're managing all this uncertainty and risk. You have to create a chimera of security and control just in order to put one foot in front of the other. The business case is nothing more than an aspiration designed to create an environment in which we can proceed into the future without really knowing what it contains.*

*

The economics used to justify the business case for HS2, to take a single example, required somebody to predict how a traveller on the railway was going to spend their time while they were travelling. If they were going to look out of the window, then the shorter the journey time the better. If they were going to work, then who cares how long they are on the train? And the calculations were based on projections of business travel growth that took no account of the impact of the Covid pandemic and the explosion of virtual meetings that has happened since. These kind of uncertainties about the benefits of a mega-project are mirrored in the opaqueness of what it will cost and how long it will take. When the Nuclear Decommissioning Authority let the contract for managing Sellafield, nobody knew what could actually be achieved in the contract period. The so-called Life-Time-Plan was used as a comfort blanket to cover the huge uncertainties. And as for the plan to integrate and test the smart metering system – which had to carry complex as-yet undefined messages, between millions of as-yet non-existent metres, through several untested communications technologies and a brand-new data management system, to every energy company in Great Britain, guarded by the largest public data security infrastructure in Europe – who in their right mind would predict how that would go?

There is a saying in the US Department of Defense about the development of major new weapons systems. They have, it is said, only two phases. The first is the 'too early to say' phase, and the second is the 'too late to change' phase. By the time you really know how much something will cost and when it will be ready, you have no alternative except the unacceptable one of leaving yourself with no weapon system at all. Veterans of Whitehall delivery will sometimes, at the end of a long and difficult day, wonder aloud whether the whole notion of a project for the most complex challenge is just plain wrong.

Each of the three business cases for the difficult, but really quite simple, Hindhead Tunnel project, will have followed a standard format mandated by the Treasury known as the Five Case Model. We don't need to go into detail, but in summary the five 'cases' explain: one, why the project makes sense strategically; two, how the economics of the chosen solution are better than the alternatives; three, where the money is coming from; four, how to procure what you need to buy; and five, how you are going to manage the project. It should all add up to a demonstration that the right project is going to be done in the right way so as to be deliverable, affordable, and provide good value for money. This sounds straightforward, but for a project like the Hindhead Tunnel, each of the business cases can run to hundreds of pages and take a small army to write.

I think there is another way to think about this kind of project, and I first came across it when I joined the Investment Committee of the UK's Department for International Development. At that time DfID's objectives were simple: reduce extreme poverty by stimulating sustainable economic development, reducing conflict and providing humanitarian aid. By law, 0.7% of national income, around £15 billion per year, was spent on pursuing this goal. Despite periodically coming under attack at home, the UK's development effort was lauded around the world and the country's commitment to aid was a matter of national pride for successive governments of all parties. The Department had a massive and enormously diverse portfolio of projects, ranging from education of girls in Pakistan to funding road construction in the Democratic Republic of Congo. I was fascinated to see how government decided which projects would receive UK funding and which not. When your aim is to make the developing world a better place, how on earth do you decide where to start? A purely economic analysis of the project to educate Pakistani girls, for example, would require you to guess how many of the girls would, as a result of their improved education, start micro-businesses, and with what economic impact. For the Congolese road project, you would have to forecast how many new jobs would be stimulated by improved transport links between Kananga and Kisangani – and what proportion of new wages would be spent on imports rather than at home. If your assumptions were right, then you could screen projects by their relative return on investment in order to decide which to fund. But the reality of international development is that you have little control over the delivery environment, and the causal relationship between inputs and outcomes is weak and unpredictable. Comparing benefit to cost ratios provides only an illusion of rigour. So how do you avoid the allocation of your £15 billion being purely random or just ideological? The answer is to use an approach known as the 'theory of change'.[1]

Developing a theory of change starts with gaining as rich as possible an understanding of the complex mix of conditions required to reduce poverty in the specific context of, say, Pakistan or the

DRC. Then you have to wrestle with the question of which of these conditions UK aid can impact most. Where are the UK's specific capabilities, and where should we leave it to others? This doesn't result in a spreadsheet of detailed analysis, but a reasoned argument for how a particular combination of UK inputs should contribute to the developed world's attempts to reach desirable outcomes. A good theory of change benefits from expert evidence, independent challenge and a diversity of opinions, and ends in something that is clear, logical and compelling. One expert uses the analogy of Google Maps –

> *this is the territory, this is how we see our bit of the territory, and this is the route that we think is best to take through it… Based on our understanding of how the territory along the route works, this is how we shall approach the journey, and these are some of the landmarks we expect to see on the way.*[2]

Now, at some point on the development journey, you do begin to need the disciplines of a project. Which roads, of how many lanes, built by whom at what cost? And do you educate girls in easy-to-reach parts of the Punjab, which will be more cost effective, or the most impoverished regions on the borders with Afghanistan, where the need is greater? But the point is that your project is justified not by the illusion of precise impact on extreme poverty, but by its contribution to a well thought through hypothesis about how the project will help.

Developing a theory of change is an imperfect science but, done well, this kind of thinking at the outset would promote much better conversations about the pros and cons of a huge government project. It would certainly be better than a long consultant-written business case that conspires to mask the real risk and uncertainty. If an open, honest and informed conversation about north-south rail connections had been held in 2010, then there would have been no headline grabbing announcement of a very specific Y-shaped network of lines, and no initiation of a project that couldn't make up its mind whether it was trying to reduce domestic air travel, shorten journey times, increase capacity, or reduce economic inequalities between London and the North. With greater clarity, but less artificial precision, maybe we would still have ended up with a project the scale and complexity of HS2 – but I doubt it. Instead, we might have pursued a series of difficult debottlenecking projects on the existing rail network. Or a portfolio of new, smaller, independent rail projects. Or projects that started in the north, not the south. We will never know, because no one ever developed a clear and compelling 'theory of change'.

Now, I am not advocating abandoning traditional business cases completely, even for the largest projects. At a certain point, and before the really big money is committed, the project should be able to state clearly what it is, how much it will cost, and how it will be delivered. For the Hindhead tunnel project that might be quite early on. But for the largest of mega-projects, it is going to be much later than ministers and officials will be comfortable with. But after the final decision has been made to invest, then we should, at least most of the time, be able to deliver the promise.

*

I cannot say whether UK international development projects still benefit from theory of change thinking. Shortly after DFID was absorbed by the Foreign and Commonwealth Office, I resigned from the investment committee when the government reneged on its commitment to spend 0.7% of GDP on aid. According to the Independent Commission for Aid Impact:

> The UK aid architecture underwent radical reorganisation with the September 2020 merger of the Department for International Development (DFID) and the Foreign and Commonwealth Office (FCO), ending 26 years of separate development and foreign ministries. The UK aid programme was also subjected to a series of drastic and highly disruptive budget reductions, as well as an extended period of budgetary uncertainty. There were also frequent changes in ministers and government priorities.[3]

Since the Commission's report was published, the Labour government has cut aid again. Nowadays, more than half of the aid money that the UK spends directly is spent in the UK, mostly on housing asylum seekers.

12

OLD CHESTNUTS

In 1995, an otherwise little-known official in the Canadian government posed the following question. 'We know why projects fail; we know how to prevent their failure – so why do they still fail?' It is known in the world of projects as Cobb's Dilemma. In the three decades since then, a whole new profession has developed to try and answer it.

My answer, for the kind of mega-projects described in this book, might be a combination of the following: flawed policy, inadequate leadership, specific outcomes being announced too early, unrealistic estimates, ineffective assurance and a systemic reluctance to face reality. Not every project suffers from every flaw. But all the projects in this book suffered from at least one, and some fell foul of many. That the problems persist, 30 years after Cobb, is not because no one has tried to solve them. A generation of government officials has put in place more processes, more procedures, more governance and more assurance. But the causes of project failure are like malaria: treatment may appear to reduce the frequency of outbreaks for a while, but the disease lingers. You will hear some say that government's project performance has improved, but there is precious little evidence for it in the largest and most challenging projects.

This chapter and the next explore why governments continue to fall into the same old traps, and what can be done about it. In them, I quote the views of current and former politicians, civil servants and delivery executives. To protect their identities, I have kept their quotations anonymous. Where the context might identify the source, I have rephrased the quotes, without changing the message.

THE POLICY

The white-collar policy stars sit in the minister's office in the evening eating pizza, then throw the policy over the balcony to the tattooed blue-collar guys with earrings to do the delivery.

Neither those who develop policy, nor those whose job is to deliver it, will like this characterisation from a long-time Whitehall watcher, but it does capture both the distance between the two populations and the disparity of esteem. To say that this is a long-standing problem is an understatement. In the sixties, a committee on the civil service, commissioned by Harold Wilson, complained about the class distinction between generalist policy mandarins and the 'scientists, engineers and other professional specialists' who were not accorded the authority that they deserved.[1] Policy professionals are at the top table. Deliverers are below the salt. A smart fast-stream recruit into the civil service policy profession may find themselves briefing ministers when they are still in their twenties. A similarly gifted project manager or commercial professional won't get to play with the big boys and girls for at least another decade.

Most projects germinate in the policy side of a department. The policy ideas are not usually all that novel. The big challenges of government are rarely completely new. The seed of an idea can lie dormant in the loam of analysis and optioneering for years. But one day, for some reason, the right combination of temperature and moisture will bring the idea to life. The problem is that the project can acquire a lot of definition, long before it gets anywhere near anybody with a delivery background. With nobody in the room who might actually have to deliver it, the risks and uncertainties are overlooked, and failure is baked into the project before it has even begun.

Getting to a policy that has a chance of becoming a healthy project requires a meeting of minds between the policy and delivery arms of a department. The 'policy stars' won't always like what the 'tattooed guys with earrings' have to say, but working together they might just find the simplification opportunities that make the policy deliverable – or be able to acknowledge that the idea, however attractive, just won't fly. A really good policy professional should be as proud of the ideas they didn't pursue as those that they did.

THE LEADERSHIP

The gulf between policy and delivery starts at the top.

> *I was at a Cabinet meeting in which each minister had to report on their major projects. One Secretary of State stood up to explain how his project was going to be finished by the date that had been announced. He had an A3 sheet showing the project phases. After everyone left the room, another Minister asked me, 'Did you believe that?' I told him that 'we haven't even defined the scope yet, and we haven't got planning permission, and we don't know what the construction phase is. So I'm afraid it was just a picture.' The Minister said, 'Thought so.' and went off quite happy with that answer.*

Delivery leaders observe that their political masters are remarkably disinterested in the gritty reality of the projects for which they are nominally responsible. Of course, backbenchers are not selected for ministerial posts because of their understanding of mega-project delivery. And the backgrounds of most ministers make them almost perversely unsuited to the subject. Recent Conservative cabinets have had a smattering of commercial experience, typically in financial services, but they were mostly made up of longstanding professional politicians. The new Labour cabinet, while also full of political lifers, has less businessmen and more lawyers and economists. But if you are hoping for political leadership that understands large scale delivery, the picture is bleak.

If delivery leaders have a low opinion of most of their political masters, the feeling is mutual. Iain Duncan Smith told the media that he had 'lost faith in the ability of the civil servants to be able to manage this [Universal Credit] programme'.[2] And when Prime Minister Sunak cancelled HS2 he took a sharp sideswipe at the leadership of the project. 'There must be some accountability for … the mismanagement of this project.'[3] If only there was decent delivery leadership, they seem to be saying, then Universal Credit would have delivered on time, and HS2 would still be on track. They are both wrong about that, but they are right that a lot of failed government projects have had underpowered delivery leadership.

The Permanent Secretaries and Directors General advising ministers are overwhelmingly from a policy background. Fewer than a quarter of permanent secretaries have a Science, Technology, Engineering or Mathematics degree. According to the Institute for Government, they are more comfortable with qualitative concepts than the numbers that underpin them.[4] Their private offices, staffed by the mandarins of the future, are full of policy generalists too. The civil service sponsor of a risky and uncertain major project is likely to be objectively underweight for the challenge.

> I would say, frankly, in government, project leaders are hugely underwhelming. I think back to the sort of crusty old project managers in industry. These were people you didn't f*** with.

Few government project deliverers have the weight, experience and charisma to generate this kind of informal authority. Taken as a whole, few would argue that the collective political, official and delivery leadership applied to the country's largest project delivery challenges is really up to the task. What makes this worse is that everybody is learning on the job.

The Institute for Government has calculated that, since 1997, ministers have typically stayed in post for less than two years. And this is the average. An ex-minister told me, 'I was the Minister for getting on for three years, but in the three years prior to me there were six if not seven ministers. How the hell can you instil confidence in supply chain partners, let alone inside the organisation.' Nick Smallwood, five years into his role leading the Infrastructure and Projects Authority, told me he was on his eighth Chief Secretary to the Treasury. This is the Cabinet minister at the centre of government who oversees public spending on projects. Several politicians told me that 'Ministers don't generally want to be associated with things that fail.' But the evidence suggests that, in fact, they are prepared to tolerate a very high degree of delivery risk – so long as it isn't likely to emerge on their watch.

Average tenures in the senior civil service are almost as short as those of ministers.[5] The Universal Credit project, which enjoyed unusually high ministerial continuity, had six accountable officials and six programme directors in its first five years. With this level of churn, relationships never have time to mature. Consequently, in the collective leadership community around a typical large project – ministers, senior civil servants, delivery executives and their sponsors – nobody trusts anybody else. A consequential characteristic of the Olympics programme was that the coalition of senior leaders, from Tessa Jowell and then Jeremy Hunt at the Cabinet table to David Higgins and John Armitt in the Olympic Delivery Authority, had time to develop confidence in each other. More usually, the relationships are somewhere on a spectrum between mutual misunderstanding and damaging toxicity. And this in turn means that for anybody who does survive for an extended period in leadership of a mega-project, the very last thing that they will ever want to do is another one. Little wonder that projects fail when everybody is an amateur, institutional memory is short, nobody trusts anybody else, and no one is around long enough to become more than theoretically accountable.

Churn in arm's length delivery bodies is lower than amongst ministers and officials. Five-year contracts with options for renewal are common. Non-executive directors and Chairs are typically signed up for three-years and their contracts are often extended. The undoubted benefits of this are undermined by the unhelpful side-effect of nourishing an unhealthy contempt amongst delivery leaders for their here-today-gone-tomorrow governors. Boards of arm's length bodies can even suffer from overlong tenures as happened in Crossrail ltd.

I can't leave the subject of leadership of mega-projects without addressing the issue of remuneration. Like it or not, people who know how to lead major projects command high salaries in the private sector. A portion of them, particularly if they are at the end of a lucrative career, are prepared to take a substantial pay cut to lead something big and important. But most, put off by the politics and the red-tape, chose to remain where they are better rewarded. In Whitehall, there is an informal and illogical benchmark set at the level of the Prime Minister's salary. It acts as a ceiling which is pierced only by a closely controlled handful. The only people in the government's army of delivery leaders who earn anything like parity with their private sector peers are a handful of arm's length body executives on projects of such high profile that the system is prepared to treat them as regrettable exceptions. These few have to suffer the annual barrage of press criticism for their remuneration when it is revealed in Annual Reports. This alone would be enough to put many people off. You often hear about a revolving door between the public and private sector, particularly in Defence. But in the major projects world it is almost always an 'exit only' door. The talent is leaving Whitehall rather than arriving.

But highly paid imports don't always flourish. Most of them struggle, at least initially, with the ambiguous political world in which they have landed, and search in vain for the clarifying simplicity of the profit drivers they are used to. And in any case, few of them have ever led a project with the level of complexity they now find themselves accountable for. Some learn and survive. Others, anchored to naive expectation that what worked for them in the private sector is bound to work here, either become ineffective or leave. The recruitment of Richard Granger, reported to be the highest paid civil servant in the country, to run the National Programme in the NHS makes the point. And his successor, who had spent twenty years in BP, was never able to wrestle successfully with the monster of a programme that Granger had created.

THE ANNOUNCEMENT

It was a slightly jaw-dropping moment because the cost was quite out there in terms of the fiscal situation we were in. Then I realised that, as far as the Minister was concerned, as soon as the announcement was made, that was the benefit. The delivery of the policy was almost secondary. I went to see the Department to check out how they intended to do all this stuff, and it was very apparent that they hadn't really worked that out. They then had to cobble together a delivery plan.

Nowhere is the gulf in worldview between ministers and deliverers starker than on the subject of project announcements. Ex-ministers repeatedly told me that they had never knowingly announced something that they knew to be unachievable. (The word 'knowingly' is doing a lot of work in these protestations. At the very outset of a project, it is hard to 'know' that something is impossible.) Deliverers are convinced that ministers don't care whether what they announce is deliverable, so long as it gets them a good headline. As for the officials in between, even though they often draft and sign-off on announcements, they tend to view them as being rather like the flu. Regrettable, but somehow inevitable. You can try to inoculate yourself from the worst of the consequences, but you can't avoid the virus altogether. 'It's not practical to tell the minister that he has to say that we don't know how long it will take', an ex-Permanent Secretary told me, 'You have to try to give them something they can say now'.

The pressure to make a project announcement can come from any number of places, but it will rarely be at a logical point in a project's development. There are moments when exposing your project to the light of day will actually support successful delivery. A purposeful announcement might help to smoke out or suppress stakeholder opposition, or formalise excluding a popular but impractical solution, or alert the supply chain to the strength of political support, or quell unrealistic expectations about when the benefits will start to flow. But this is probably not what prompts the announcement. It is more likely to serve a political purpose. Take the announcement of 'Network North' made by Prime Minister Sunak in an attempt to blunt the impact of cancelling HS2.

No government has ever developed a more ambitious scheme for Northern Transport than our new Network North... You will be able to get from Manchester to

the new station in Bradford in 30 minutes, Sheffield in
42 minutes, and to Hull in 84 minutes on a fully electri-
fied line.[6]

The so-called Network North scheme had been cobbled together in
secret in the Department for Transport in a few weeks. The officials
who wrote it were not allowed to talk to anyone in Network Rail.
Most of the rail projects in it had already been announced but none
of them had an approved business case.

Sometimes, project announcements are prompted by something
completely unrelated.

> *It may be that there is something horrible going on within*
> *the Department and they'll say, 'We've got to put some-*
> *thing out, something positive I can talk about'. Or it could*
> *be that Number 10 calls to say, 'Can anyone put anything*
> *into the grid. We just need to have a statement made in the*
> *House of Commons now about something. Has anyone*
> *got anything they can say?'.*

But there is another impetus for ministerial and prime-ministerial
announcements that is under-appreciated by officials and deliverers.
They are a symptom of the lack of trust the political class has in its
bureaucracy. In 2019, Prime Minister Johnson described the government's 2033 target for rolling out full-fibre broadband to every
part of the UK as 'laughably unambitious' and he announced that
instead it would be complete in 2025.

> *In the mind of the Prime Minister, announcements were*
> *used to increase the level of ambition in the Department.*
> *It was an expression of prime ministerial impatience. He*
> *announced 2025 when all the advice to him was that it*
> *was impossible. But he was doing it to say, 'Pull your fin-*
> *ger out!'*

Announcements like this, that place specifics of the scope, time,
or cost on the record, when they are unsupported by delivery plans,
or before the project has developed to the point of being able to
make an accurate assessment, are always over-optimistic. As we
saw with Universal Credit, and again with the Smart Meter project,

the scale and benefits will be front and centre, but the risks and uncertainties will be nowhere to be seen.

Why are ministers allowed to get away with it? In a conversation with a Whitehall official, I tried to draw a parallel with the longstanding tradition that ministers must not mislead Parliament.

> *If a minister tells an untruth in the House, they have to face up and explain, the moment they realise they've done it. And they might well have to resign. So how is it acceptable to make claims about future investments which don't stand up to scrutiny. Shouldn't that be as big a crime as telling a lie?*

He looked at me slightly pityingly and said, 'Well you can't prove it's a lie until years later when it turns out to be a lie, can you?'

THE ESTIMATES

> *There's so much reason for me to low-ball it – to understate the costs and overstate the benefits. Obviously I'm not doing it, but don't underestimate the ability of the human brain to do a bit of gymnastics to justify what it wants to believe. There's every incentive on me to play the system, because I know that if the Treasury gives us what we've asked for the next financial year, then we're on the conveyor belt. So there is no incentive for me to say 'well I think it's four billion pounds, but it might actually be nearer six or seven billion'. I'd just be signing the death warrant for the project.*

In 2024, the short-lived Labour Transport Secretary Louise Haigh briefed the press on the cost of completing the remnants of HS2. 'The costs of HS2 have been allowed to spiral out of control but since becoming Transport Secretary I have seen up close the scale of failure in project delivery – and it's dire.'[7] The post-mortem on the delivery of HS2 has not been carried out yet. Time will tell how dire it has been. But is Haigh right that the costs 'have been allowed to spiral out of control'? The implication is that with competent management the project should have been delivered for the original estimate. But is that true?

In fact, building *this particular* railway, with its extraordinary speed requirements, long tunnels and extreme straightness, constrained by *these* planning and environmental regulations, with their insistence on kilometre long bat-protection tunnels, during a pandemic and the subsequent inflation, was always going to cost something like it is actually costing. It was certainly not going to come in at the original budget. What has spiralled is not so much the cost as the gap between what was estimated and what is now forecast. The problem Haigh is alluding to is not really with the cost, but with the original estimate. Approving unrealistic cost and schedule estimates plays a big part in most mega-project failures. How can that be? Why do we so often underestimate how long projects will take and how much they will cost?

If you are leading a large public sector project, this is how your cost forecasts will be put together. (Schedule forecasts follow a very similar process.) The starting point is a base cost estimate if everything goes perfectly to plan. This is a sort of macro version of the 'if it takes three men four days to dig a trench five yards long...' type of estimate. But everyone knows that not everything will go to plan. So your project team will create a register of the problems the project might have to cope with through its life. Each of these risks is allocated a potential impact in pounds (and months) and a likelihood of it occurring. All of this data is fed into a computer that does some fancy mathematics to combine all the risks and give a probabilistic distribution of outcomes. This is called a Quantified Risk Analysis, QRA, and developing it can become quite a project in its own right. A profession of Risk Managers has grown up to administer this kind of exercise, and specialist consultancies will offer to do it for you. The outputs will be presented to you with the authority of unbiased fact. 'There's a 50% likelihood the project will be completed for £1.4 billion and a 70% chance of it costing less than £1.55 billion.' Unfortunately, this façade of precision masks a mountain of bias.

To start with, the base cost estimate will be flaky, particularly early on. The precise scope will not yet be clear, and the cost inputs are likely to come from suppliers who are very keen for the project to go ahead. The base cost uncertainty is certain to be underplayed. And your risk register is nothing more than a list of guesses about what might go wrong and with what likelihood. The QRA is less an objective analysis and more an exercise of imagination and experience. As a senior defence executive told me, 'The more experience you bring to bear, the less viable your project becomes.' So with your base cost underestimated and the uncertainty and risk in your project played down, (and the same biases affecting the schedule estimates), the forecasts included in your early business cases are, to say the very least, optimistic. If a premature political announcement has already put an unrealistic estimate into the public domain, your first formal estimate will be even lower. The later business cases, probably put together by your successors, will be tethered to your estimates, leading them to have to choose – either take the punishment meted out for letting the cost of the project 'spiral out of control', or continue with the delusion.

The institutional environment into which your estimate is presented really doesn't help. Sometimes, under the influence of the inverse square law, your minister may make no effort at all to understand what it takes to deliver your projects. One ex-minister told me that 'the time it takes to build a railway station is just ridiculous. When flooding happened and the army were brought in, they erected a station in less than a month.' Or your minister will suspect that you are padding the estimate to make your life easier. 'The project will set itself a target they really think they can hit, because – why wouldn't they?' And it won't only be ministers who look through the wrong end of the telescope. I remember sitting in debates in the Cabinet Office and Treasury in the early years of HS2, when the cost estimates were still in the low tens of billions. Armed with naive comparisons with France's high-speed rail projects, the officials were incredulous at the figures HS2 Ltd were proposing. Consequently, the whole debate was not framed as, 'Are we sure that it can be done for that?' but, 'How can it possibly cost that much?' Needless to say, the estimates subsequently reduced.

The underlying problem is the unbroken alignment of perverse incentives from top to bottom. When Prime Minister Johnson approved the Notice to Proceed for the first phase of HS2, every layer of governance below him – Transport Secretary, Department

Officials and HS2 Ltd itself – was desperate for the project to go ahead, not to mention the civil contractors on the point of signing huge deals. Everyone is incentivised to believe in a low estimate. It is known in the project world as 'limbo-dancing', and it is endemic in large public sector projects.

The Treasury calls this tendency to underestimate cost and schedule 'optimism bias', which makes it sound like a generic and rather endearing example of the kind of cognitive kink that all human beings are subject to. In fact, it is a systematic but unspoken conspiracy to get projects sanctioned by collective self-deception.

> *Getting projects approved is a huge uphill battle. The only way to jump the hurdles is to make the project look as low risk, as economically attractive, and as affordable as possible.*

THE ASSURANCE

When the fault lines in a mega-project, so obvious in retrospect, begin to appear, the question I am most often asked is, 'How on earth did it get approved? Didn't somebody check?'. In fact, too many people doing too much checking might just be part of the problem.

Over the years, more and more governance layers, audits, reviews and checks have been built into project approvals in repeated attempts to prevent the failures of the past being repeated. By the time a mega-project reaches the desk of the Chief Secretary of the Treasury, it will probably have been picked over nine or ten times. Its meandering journey through the arm's length body, the sponsor organisation, the department, the Cabinet Office and the Treasury may have taken twelve to fifteen months, and sometimes much longer. Before it is finally approved, the project will go round this assault course three times at the Strategic, Outline and Final business case stages. Conservatively, that makes around thirty opportunities for scrutiny and checking. If it is your project, the time burden on you is severe and takes you away from making real progress. But if you want your project to fly, then the bureaucratic

tradecraft required to clear the approval obstacles is more important than anything else.

You might think that all this examination will lead to a thor-
oughly assured business case by the time it gets its final approval.
In fact, the effect is quite likely to be the reverse. Each of the 9 or
10 boards and committees, faced with a long complex business
case, knows that it has passed multiple hurdles already and will
have to clear more before it is approved. The incentive to get properly to grips with its strategic, economic, commercial and project
management complexities is not strong. If there was a big problem, surely someone would have picked it up by now. So the tyres
will be kicked and some partially informed questions will be asked
before the project moves on to the next stage. Sometimes approval
will follow a mandated assurance review. At their best, reviews like
these can drive up the likelihood of successful delivery by bringing
difficult issues to the surface so they can be addressed. This requires
real-world experience and the intuition to distinguish between the
main conundrums that need calling out and the white noise of
problems that accompany every large project. Assurers also need
the courage to be explicit about their judgements, even when their
findings are uncomfortable and inconvenient for senior officials
and ministers. Unfortunately, most government assurance is not
like this. Most of the checking will focus not on whether the best
decisions are being proposed, but whether all the right processes
have been followed and the right boxes ticked. All that poor assurance achieves is nit-picking, sugar-coating, or crying wolf at the
expense of bureaucracy and delay. If really effective assurance does
occur at any point, its findings are likely either to be drowned out
by the volume of less valuable checking, or else to fall on deaf ears.

THE DENIAl

*Maybe were not good enough at preparing people for how
to do it, but there are ways of delivering bad news. People
taking on these roles need to be prepared and trained and
capable of delivering robust advice and robust messages.
And ministers need to understand that it is their job to*

*hear them. You don't have to take the advice, but you sure
as hell have to listen to it.*

A well-respected ex-minister told me that, 'No civil servant can go
wrong if they just lay out for the Minster exactly where a project
is and where the problems are.' But when I quoted that to a battle-
scarred veteran of delivery he scoffed. 'Try saying that to Gavin
Williamson!' A younger civil servant, faced with advice to speak
up, said, 'It's alright for you. You don't have a bloody mortgage.'

If the now approved project has been built on untested policy,
is being managed by a succession of ill-equipped politicians and
officials, suffers from a prematurely announced and over-specific
definition of success, and has a low-balled and poorly assured business case, it is little wonder that at some point during delivery the
signs of impending failure begin to emerge.

If you are running the delivery body when the symptoms start
to show, command feels less like leading an army into battle, and
more like working under siege. You feel surrounded by hostile
forces and your erstwhile allies are nowhere to be seen. Political
support becomes more grudging as the upside of announcement
recedes into the past and ribbon-cutting is still years away. The
Department's attention has moved on to the priorities of the next
set of ministers who are sure to have arrived since your project
was approved. Your departmental sponsors, caught between the
practical realities of delivery and the political realities of government, begin to check and challenge your every decision and progress report. Nobody wants to take bad news up the chain. You
begin to regard central government assurance not as an opportunity for helpful fresh eyes, but as an attack to be repulsed. A critical Cabinet Office review can bury you in a bureaucratic tsunami
of work. Outside of government, the project's critics are much
more newsworthy than its supporters. Select committees give MPs
the opportunity to make headlines at your expense. Meanwhile a
National Audit Office review into the project, and the inevitable
Public Accounts Committee hearings that will follow it, loom in
the project calendar like a colonoscopy appointment.

Surrounded, it seems, by foes, the arm's length body becomes a
fortress, sealed as far as possible from incoming fire, and endlessly

projecting as positive a picture as possible. Defending the stronghold is a huge distraction. Navigating the next assurance review, preparing for the select committee, and securing next year's funding, are always the most proximate leadership challenges. But inside the fortress, the realities of delivery are emerging. Project leaders may find that, in an attempt to make up time lost in tortuous approval or planning processes, they have started construction too soon, before the design is sufficiently stable to prevent re-design and rework. Or they have lost control of changes to the scope, letting their contractors off the contractual hook. Or the consequences of complexity are coming home to roost. Soon, the cost and schedule forecasts begin to grow, eating into the project's contingency. Initially, messages into government are carefully hedged to prevent a bow-wave of ever more defending, explaining and excusing. But eventually the scale of the problems becomes evident for everyone to see.

At some stage, reality has to be faced in the Department and the centre of government. It may be early on, as in the Olympics programme, or at five minutes to midnight, as happened in Crossrail. But before that, there is probably going to be a further period of denial while one or more levers are pulled to try to bring the project back onto plan. The first lever launches a frantic hunt for unicorns – new ideas that will make the cost and schedule realities go away. A 'red-team' will invade the project to find the opportunities that the project leaders have been too dense to spot. The second lever parachutes a white knight into the project – a superhero who will rescue it from its failing path. Ministers did this twice on the Universal Credit project, firstly installing the CEO of the Major Projects Authority and then a construction executive from the 2012 Olympics programme. Neither lasted long. The most desperate lever will be a surreptitious attempt to redefine the project completion milestone into something that can be met on time. In 2018, Crossrail wasted weeks looking at whether a part-time shuttle service could be opened between Abbeywood and Canary Wharf while the rest of the railway could be completed in the background.

Unicorn hunts, white knights, and goalpost-shifting usually achieve little more than delaying the inevitable. While the fruits of failure may only be visible now, their roots go deep into the past.

Once a large project has gone off the rails there is no way to bring it back on track. The only question is when and how to acknowledge that the announced dates and budget cannot be met, and what approach to take to resetting the business case. In principle this is the opportunity to take stock of everything that has been learnt about the project since it was initiated, to acknowledge the remaining uncertainties, to be realistic about how many of the remaining risks can be mitigated, and to replan with enough float and contingency to allow the project to be completed in a controlled manner. You can tell whether you have done that because if you have then the contractors' committed cost and schedule forecasts should fit comfortably within the arm's length body's approved envelope, and the government's new business case should have contingency for the risks and uncertainties that have yet to emerge.

But that will almost certainly not happen. The incentives that led to limbo-dancing in the first place will conspire again to force the smallest cost escalation and schedule slippage possible. The justification will be that you need to keep the pressure on to avoid everyone taking their foot of the gas. This is how the operational date for the Home Office's enormously complex mobile communications project for the blue-light services slipped to 2022, then 2024, and now stands at 2026. It is a way of guaranteeing that a failed project remains a failure right up until the end.

13

CANDOUR, CLARITY, RIGOUR

When I arrived in Whitehall in 2007, there was already a prescription to resolve Cobb's Dilemma. It was called the 'NAO/OGC Common Causes of Project Failure'. You can look them up.[1] If you could avoid them, your project would succeed. There was even a phase where the Treasury required senior officials to certify that they had banished the common causes from their projects as a condition of approval. Whitehall has, since then, produced any number of prescriptions for avoiding project failure. For what it is worth, here is another one.

1. Delivery should have parity of esteem with policy in Government.

2. Ministers and Senior Civil Servants should spend much longer in post.

3. Delivery challenges should be matched by the capability of delivery leadership, even if that means paying market-competitive remuneration.

4. Weeding out poor performers in the public sector should be much easier.

5. Projects should not be initiated without clarity on what they are to achieve.

6. Announcements with specific predictions of scope, cost and time should not be made until the project is sufficiently developed to make them realistic.

7. Deliverable simplicity should trump theoretically perfect complexity in the development of projects.

8. Cost and Schedule estimates should take account of uncertainty and risk, even though ranges will be very wide until the project is well developed.

9. Project approval should be simpler and swifter, with less, but better assurance which focuses on outcome delivery rather than process compliance.

10. Unanticipated pressures on cost and schedule should be acknowledged early.

My list, like all the others, may be worthy. But unless we can change the structures and incentives that surround major projects, it is also worthless.

If you glued these, and the OGC Common Causes, into a scrapbook, together with all the other review recommendations made over the years, and then added the wisdom of project management academia, it would still not look like rocket-science. In the last two decades, Project Management has developed into a full-blown profession with qualifications, ethical standards and a professional body. But the fundamental success factors for projects remain, at heart, a matter of applied common sense. The problem is that all the tendencies shaping the environment in which public sector projects are conceived, approved, and delivered drive the opposite of common sense. We will not improve the record of delivery for huge government projects unless we can tilt the incentives away from disingenuousness, ambiguity, and laxity towards candour, clarity and rigour.

*

Three anonymised fragments: The first is an ex-minster complaining about obfuscation by his officials.

> *What I got back was completely hopeless. It was irrelevant and didn't get near to an answer. I was so enraged I managed to get hold of the entire email chain. That revealed*

that the person to whom the question had been sent – who was at the bottom of the pecking list – produced a perfect answer. It was honest, it was direct, it told me exactly what I wanted to know. But then it had been through count-less hands that had 'improved' on the answer. Not only had the answer changed, but there had also been email exchanges about what information they should share with me. If we share this with him, it will lead to that …'. Until eventually the answer comes, and it is completely unus-able. If they'd only given me the first answer…

The second is a permanent secretary-level official describing the pressure to support an unjustified claim.

The Minister could stand up and say, 'We're going to build this amazing thing. It's going to be really hard, it's going to take a long time, and it's going to cost more than we think'. But that's not how it's going to work. They're going to say, 'This is brilliant and it's going to be quicker than we could imagine'. And if anybody says, 'Hold on that's really not very likely', or 'How are we actually going to do it?' then they're seen as unhelpful.*

The third comes from an ex-board member in an arm's length body.

We had a board meeting to decide whether or not to accept the budget. I phoned the Chair and said, 'I'm sorry, I don't believe the numbers. I think we're £1.8 billion short'. For the board it was an on/off switch, you either accepted and made the best of it, or not, and brought on a whole lot of nausea. The board accepted it. I resigned at that point. We've created an environment where the incen-tives through the system are to do the wrong thing. And it takes courage and financial independence for people to do the right thing.

---

*For a senior civil servant, 'unhelpful' is code for 'career limiting'.

If you only spoke with civil servants, you would conclude that the problem is all down to the politicians. A senior official in the centre of government rolled off to me a list of ministers who were open to hearing bad news and those who 'don't want to know'. For every name in the first list, there were three in the second. But in truth, civil servants and delivery leaders are complicit. When the Crossrail board sat on the reality of the state of their project until the truth became undeniable, it wasn't because of a politician. When a Secretary of State showed his Cabinet colleagues a fictitious picture of how his project was going to be completed, he hadn't written the PowerPoint himself. His officials had done it for him.

> *Civil servants talk about speaking truth unto power, but my experience is that they rarely do it. And to be fair, some ministers have extreme reactions to being told that what they want to do can't be done.*

It is a poor excuse, but a defence nonetheless, to say that realism in delivery is not a simple matter of telling the truth and avoiding a lie. Deliverability is not binary; it is an informed judgement made despite uncertainty. But this smokescreen cannot obscure the fact that a culture has grown up in which it is acceptable to mislead through half-truths and obfuscations. Far from being on an improving curve, this tendency may in recent years have actually got worse.

> *After Brexit, Trump and Johnson, I found myself very uncomfortable in the public sector where I saw a behaviour which is very Boris – cakism and boosterism. 'Just be positive, talk big and be optimistic. That's how you incentivise and motivate people.'*

The stark fact is that it has become collectively acceptable for everyone in the system to shirk their professional accountability. Any penalty for dodging the truth is dwarfed by the imperative of serving the assumed short-term interests of the minister, disguising an embarrassing truth, ducking a difficult conversation, or clearing the next approval hurdle. A well-developed ability to surf ambiguity in order to avoid acknowledging an unacceptable reality might even be a key career strength.

I am convinced that changing these incentives is the key to unlocking the door to better project delivery performance. It won't be easy, and it won't be quick. There will be growing pains and false starts. It will mean confronting some longstanding shibboleths about how government works. But if we can't change the culture that surrounds mega-projects, we will hinder our attempts as a nation to face up to our challenges: productivity, debt, growth, national security and climate change. What follows will not be enough on its own. The old chestnuts (ministerial tenure, civil-service churn, delivery and commercial capability, the unhelpful Prime Minister salary benchmark...) will have to be addressed as well. But no amount of improvement in these will prevent project failure if everyone involved is motivated to do the wrong thing.

My prescription for change has five elements: an enforced duty of candour; an explicit differentiation between announcements and investment decisions; bureaucratic rigour about these decisions, with proper records of business cases, and the evidence and assurance opinions on which they have been based; a step-change in the quality of external scrutiny; and finally, a Whitehall-wide strengthening of the functions essential to successful project delivery.

AN ENFORCED DUTY OF CANDOUR

Someone told me that everyone involved in leading major projects should be made to take some kind of Hippocratic Oath to tell the truth. But in fact, most of them already have. The civil service code requires advice to ministers to be 'on the basis of the evidence, and accurately present the options and facts', without ignoring counter evidence even if it is inconvenient or unhelpful to the argument.[2] And most professionals in arm's length bodies, whether directors on the board or project managers and commercial professionals in the field, have a duty to provide accurate, relevant and timely information to their shareholders and stakeholders. So almost everyone below ministerial level is bound by a duty of candour. Ministers, it is true, only have to be honest in Parliament. But those who

knowingly mislead the House have to offer their resignation to
the Prime Minister, and when they give evidence to parliamentary
committees, they have to make sure that their civil servants are 'as
helpful as possible in providing accurate, truthful and full information'.[3] So is the answer for public servants simply to toughen
up and remember their professional accountabilities? It would be
naive to expect this to be sufficient. This book is full of examples of
unpunished economies with the truth, and a breach of professional
code has to be egregious before a professional body will sanction a
member. Something more is required.

A few years ago, there was a change to the accountability of
project owners in Whitehall whereby they were required to account
directly to parliamentary committees for the decisions and actions
they take to deliver their project.[4] I have to say that I have wit-
nessed virtually no effect of this change, with a single exception.
When presented with a policy change proposal from his minister
which would have increased his risk of delivery, this one civil servant told the minister that they would of course comply, but that
their accountability to Parliament would require them to write to
the Chair of the Public Accounts Committee informing her that the
change would increase the risk to successful delivery of the project.
The policy change was quietly dropped. A counterweight is required
to tilt the incentives so as to make this kind of candour the norm
rather than the exception.

Whether you are leading, delivering, governing or assuring a
major project, you need to feel that if you dodge reality or fudge
your professional judgement, you are going to be held to account.

ANNOUNCEMENTS VERSUS DECISIONS

*The Minister called us when we were in a car. He asked,
'How much do you think it's going to cost?' and the head
of procurement said, 'I haven't got a clue, how quickly do
you want the answer?' The Minister wanted it by the end
of the day. 'I'm going to say it tomorrow. So, give me your
best estimate now.' So we gave him the advice, properly
caveated. We were basically sucking our finger and waving*

it in the air, but he used the number anyway. And some-
how it became the truth. 'You said £800 million, what do
you mean that it's £1.3 billion. Why has it changed?'

The Labour Party manifesto for the 2024 general election included a commitment to decarbonise the UK's electricity grid by 2030. Later in the year, Prime Minister Starmer softened the pledge somewhat to 95% of power being carbon-free. Few people with deep knowledge of the UK's electrical infrastructure think that this is feasible. But it is unrealistic to expect politicians to qualify every stretching ambition with a realism statement. (Imagine JFK's Chief of Staff asking him to say, 'I believe that this nation should commit itself to achieving the goal, before this decade is out, of landing a man on the moon and returning him safely to the earth…. *but we don't know whether it's feasible and it will probably take longer…*'.) But, having stated the overarching goal, how should the government treat the individual decarbonisation projects underpinning it without setting them up to fail? I think the solution to this puzzle lies in a new institutional insistence on clarity about the difference between an announcement and a decision.

When Labour Transport Secretary Andrew Adonis unveiled HS2 in 2009, with great specificity about its route, train speeds, journey times, costs and opening dates, it may have been a statement of government policy, but was it a project investment decision? When, three days after the 2024 election was called, Health Secretary Steve Barclay recommitted a future Tory government to building forty new hospitals by 2030, it may have been a manifesto pledge, but was it a project investment decision? In both cases, commentators reported them as such, but in fact, the announcements themselves were not decisions, but points on a spectrum somewhere between aspiration and daydream.

This confusion is poisonous. Announcements and formal investment decisions are both valid and valuable things – but they are not the same. If unevidenced announcements are treated like investment decisions, the seeds of future project failure are sown right at the beginning. The incentives in the system to crowbar the scope, cost and schedule of an emerging project into a predetermined envelope become irresistible.

The answer is to differentiate explicitly between the two. Countless HS2 announcements were made in the decade after Andrew Adonis's White Paper, but the investment decision to proceed wasn't made until 2020, and then only for the first phase. And decisions for most of the 40 hospitals still haven't been made. A formal investment decision is a meaningful commitment to proceed. It is not irreversible, but is much stronger than any preceding announcement. Even Prime Minister Sunak's decision to cancel HS2 didn't reverse the Phase One investment decision Prime Minister Johnson had made in 2020.

Currently, there is an unhelpful inequality of perception. Announcements are widely reported as though they were decisions. Actual decisions happen on a different timescale and rarely see the light of day. In her October 2024 budget statement, Chancellor Rachel Reeves announced that the government would fund taking HS2 right into central London rather than terminating it at Old Oak Common. The media has taken this to be a firm decision. It was not. It was a statement of policy.

Publishing formal investment decisions would correct this imbalance and refocus the external world on what is actually decided. It would undermine the tendency for ministers and media alike to feel that once a project is announced, a firm commitment to scope, time and cost has been made, leaving only the mundane business of delivery ahead. Journalists have a role to play here, but getting to this clarity and openness also requires something else. It needs officialdom to bring much more rigour to the bureaucratic niceties of decision making.

BUREAUCRATIC RIGOUR

While I was researching the projects for this book, I asked a contact in the Cabinet Office to pull out some of the original business cases. They were nowhere to be found. This wasn't the result of a conspiracy to conceal what had been decided, but simply that Whitehall is bizarrely poor at filing. Investment decisions are a hurdle that a project must clear, but once over it the system simply doesn't place any importance on recording exactly what has been decided. This sloppiness contributes to the sense that what is important is not what was promised at the point of decision, but what was most recently announced. If the project schedule is coming under pressure, then perhaps the Minister could begin to say that the service will be available 'from' the promised date rather than 'by' the promised date. Perhaps the number of aircraft will no longer be 'x' but become 'up-to x'. Over time, without an explicit reaffirmation of the decision to invest, the scope of the project, and its cost and schedule, drift away from what was formally sanctioned. There are pockets of greater diligence, but generally speaking the disciplines of record keeping are shrouded in bureaucratic fog. And it is hard to hold anyone to account for a business case that you can't find, or which exists in multiple different versions, or a change to which has been approved but not filed. Nobody feels on the hook for what was originally decided.

The official record of the business case itself should be accompanied by formal submissions of the evidence upon which it relies, including cost and schedule forecasts and the assumptions that underpin them. The names of the professionals who sign them off should be recorded too, together with their opinion about the risks and uncertainties attached to their judgements. Assurance opinions should be included as well, again with the names of the assurers documented. With exceptions along the lines of those in the Freedom of Information Act, and redactions for commercial sensitivity, the project approval file should be available to the public and the press. If the project scope does indeed change, or it requires more time and money, then it should be formally and openly re-sanctioned. This is not the sexiest proposal I have ever made, but this level of rigour would nudge the balance of incentives in support of those professionals who want to stand behind their genuine professional judgements and inhibit the others who are, today, submitting to the institutional pressure to fudge.

EXTERNAL SCRUTINY

The National Audit Office, at least with regard to its work on major projects, is an under-acknowledged national treasure. Their value for money reports bring the dry unemotional outlook of an auditor to the task of assessing of what has gone wrong. Their reports are a treasure trove of insight and experience. Few private sector companies or academic institutions have a better stockpile of learning. But, like all audits, their assessments are after the fact. And the Public Accounts Committee meetings that follow them, feared as they are by public servants, serve the traditional auditing role of visiting the battlefield after the fighting and bayonetting the wounded. When the project is originally sanctioned, this ordeal is generally far in the future.

Even with more candour and rigour, there is no getting away from the fact that everybody approving, sponsoring, delivering, and assuring major projects is working for the government. Something genuinely independent is required. Whether it is an extension of the role of the National Audit Office, or a project delivery equivalent of the Office for Budget Responsibility, something is needed to fill this gap. Small, experienced and above all independent, it should scrutinise investment decisions for the largest projects of government and provide an independent judgement about deliverability. It would no doubt be as unpopular with some ministers as the OBR has been with those who want to follow their political intuition rather than independent and authoritative analysis of the UK's public finances.

Finally, Parliament should find a way to make Select Committee scrutiny of projects much more effective. Using Joint Committees of both Houses in order to professionalise and depoliticise their scrutiny would probably help, as would supporting them with advice from people with more professional delivery experience.

STRONGER FUNCTIONS

In 2011, David Cameron wrote to his Cabinet colleagues about 'common and unacceptable failings in projects which we simply cannot repeat'.[5] His letter included yet another list of the causes of failure:

> *Unrealistically tight timescale; Lack of Business Case*
> *to establish absolute goals; Scope not finalised prior to*

Project start; Incomplete specification before procurement
commences; Absence of, or limited, options analysis; No
agreed budget or contingency planning; No implementa-
tion or strategic risk management plan; Weak commercial
and contract management capability.

Sound familiar? The letter gave prime ministerial authority to a new, stronger, mandate for the Major Projects Authority – the new name for my old directorate in the Office of Government Projects. It required, to give a single example, 'a Starting Gate review ... to assess the deliverability of all major new initiatives before project delivery gets underway'. The MPA was empowered to write to the Prime Minister's office with 'any instances of non-compliance'. I would have killed for such a mandate when I was in the Office of Government Commerce. But compliance with the decree mandating Starting Gates lasted about five minutes.

It is a perennial problem in Whitehall that well-intentioned but incremental reforms and improvements never get a chance to take root before they are overtaken by new priorities or reorganisations. Take my Major Projects Directorate in the Office of Government Commerce in the Treasury. Since I left it in 2009, it has been relocated into an Efficiency and Reform Group in the Cabinet Office, rebranded as the Major Projects Authority, merged with Infrastructure UK and rebranded again as the Infrastructure and Projects Authority, and is shortly to be moved back into the Treasury and merged again with the National Infrastructure Commission to become the National Infrastructure and Strategic Transformation Authority. An insider paraphrased the Chief Secretary to the Treasury's announcement of the latest change to me as, 'We're going to fix infrastructure, we're going to accelerate, it's all going to go faster, it's all going to be better.'

You will be hard pressed to find anybody who thinks that the centre of government works well. In recent years, there have been any number of remedies proposed by think-tanks, commissions and reviews. The Institute for Government advocates putting the civil service on a stronger statutory basis, with a Civil Service Board, including independent non-executives, to set standards.[6] Lord Maude, once David Cameron's Cabinet Office Minister, wants to see a Head of the Civil Service, separate from the Cabinet Secretary, recruited from the private sector, and an independent regulator to hold the service to account.[7] Others have recommended a Department of the Prime Minister and Cabinet, on the New Zealand model, which merges No.10 with parts of the Cabinet Office. And numerous parties want to dilute the power of the Treasury by moving responsibility for spending to a new Department for Growth. Machinery of government changes are not my specialist subject, except to say that in my experience the benefits they intend seem always to be lost in the distraction they cause. But there is one innovation I do think should be pursued in the interests of better delivery.

A typical large private sector company organisation is a matrix which balances the authority of business executives, such as a Chief Operating Officer, with that of central functional directors: Chief Finance Officer, HR Director, Chief Procurement Officer, Chief Information Officer, and so on. The mix of solid lines and dotted lines will fluctuate over time, but for the matrix to be effective requires real functional power. The corporate centre doesn't need to be big, but it does needs to be impactful. In government, the functions are simply too weak. So I favour structural and sustainable strengthening of the professions which are critical to project delivery, in particular finance, commercial, procurement, digital and project management. The centre of government needs a weighty presence from the voice of experienced, hard-nosed, deliverers.

Stronger functions would uphold the standards of professional competence and ethics, including the duty of candour. They would provide institutional support for professionals standing up to the pressure to underestimate risk and uncertainty, and consequences for those who don't. They would recruit, shape and develop the talent in the function, placing the right people into the right projects, and leaving them there long enough to make progress. A strong function can become the repository of good practice and structured learning from experience, and a guide for introduction of new techniques and technologies.

Strict constitutionalists worry about diluting the accountability of the Secretary of State and the Permanent Secretary if the functions are too strong. But the reality is that, when the largest projects fail, they are a problem for the whole of government, not just the department. The delivery accountability in departments needs to be matched by much more effective functional challenge and support.

*

If, in the course of your reading, I have left you with the impression that if only we had different people, or different processes, or different structures in government, then delivering large public sector projects would be easy, I would like to correct that now. None of the failed projects I have described in this book, nor any of the others that I could have included instead, is anything but a monumental challenge. Delivering huge projects will always be hard. There will always be failures as well as successes. The stories I have told do feature the odd villain – a self-serving minister, an incompetent civil servant, an arrogant or spineless delivery leader. But most of those involved in these massive endeavours, including the unsung thousands of engineers, designers, project managers, lawyers and commercial professionals in departments, arm's length bodies and the supply chain, are doing their best in a system that isn't working.

In this book I have described eight mega-projects: HS2, Crossrail, Restoration and Renewal, Universal Credit, the Smart Meter project, Astute Submarines, Sellafield outsourcing, and the National Programme in the NHS. Together, they represent investment that is greater than the combined annual budgets of the Departments for Defence, Transport, Education, and Culture, Media and Sport. I could have chosen any number of other projects: the Emergency Services Network project, the Identity Cards scheme, the project for Aircraft Carriers, or the project for the aircraft to fly from them.

We simply must do better. The structures and incentives that are at the root of project failure must be addressed. Closing the delivery gap is an imperative for the UK government as important as any of the other great challenges of statesmanship.

NOTES

CHAPTER 1

1. Prime Minister Rishi Sunak. Speech to the Conservative Party Conference. 4 October 2023.

2. National Audit Office. HS2: update following cancellation of Phase 2. 2024. Page 4.

3. National Audit Office. HS2: update following cancellation of Phase 2. 2024.

4. Eddington R, Sir. The Eddington Transport Study. The Case for Action: Sir Rod Eddington's advice to government. 2006. Para 1.142.

5. Institute for Government. Stephen Glaister. HS2: Levelling up or the pursuit of an icon? 2021. Page 15.

6. Department for Transport. High Speed Rail - White Paper. 2010.

7. Institute for Government. Stephen Glaister. HS2: Levelling up or the pursuit of an icon? 2021. Page 23.

8. Philip Georgiadis, Jim Pickard, and Gill Plimmer. HS2 spent £100mn on tunnel to protect rare bats. Financial Times. 7 November 2024.

9. Douglas Oakervee (Chair). Oakervee Review of HS2. 2019. Page 30. https://www.gov.uk/government/publications/oakervee-review-of-hs2

10. National Audit Office. HS2: update following cancellation of Phase 2. 2024. Page 4.

CHAPTER 3

1. London Assembly Plenary Meeting: Thursday 6 September 2018. Transcript of Item 11.a – Question and answer Session: Delay to Crossrail. Page 1.

2. London Assembly. Transport Committee. April 2019. Derailed: Getting Crossrail back on track. Page 13.

3. Crossrail Learning Legacy. Crossrail Ltd. https://learninglegacy. crossrail.co.uk/

4. Department for Transport. Press Release. July 13 2018. Secretary of State appoints Sir Terry Morgan as new HS2 Ltd Chairman. https://www.gov.uk/government/news/secretary-of-state-appoints-sir-terry-morgan-as-new-hs2-ltd-chairman

5. London Assembly. Transport Committee. April 2019. Derailed: Getting Crossrail back on track. Page 17.

CHAPTER 4

1. Caroline Shenton. *The Day Parliament Burned Down*. Oxford University Press. 2012.

2. Study Group appointed by the Management Boards of both Houses of Parliament. Restoration and Renewal of the Palace of Westminster: Pre-feasibility Study and Preliminary Strategic Business case. 2012. Page 5.

3. House of Lords/House of Commons. Joint Committee on the Palace of Westminster. Restoration and Renewal of the Palace of Westminster. First Report of Session 2016–17. 8 September 2016.

4. Statement of Impact. Draft Parliamentary Buildings (Restoration and Renewal) Bill. 2019.

5. Study Group appointed by the Management Boards of both Houses of Parliament. Restoration and Renewal of the Palace of Westminster: Pre-feasibility Study and Preliminary Strategic Business case. 2012. Page 6.

6. Hansard. House of Commons. Restoration and Renewal (Report of the Joint Committee). Debated on 31 January 2018.

7. UK Parliament. House of Lords Library. The restoration and renewal programme: Recent developments and next steps. 22 September 2023. Page 3.

8. Reported to the Author by a member of the Programme Board.

CHAPTER 5

1. The Centre for Social Justice. Dynamic Benefits: Towards welfare that works. A Policy Report from the Economic Dependency Working Group. Chaired by Dr Stephen Brien. September 2009.

2. David Freud's account of his time as Minister of State for Welfare Reform, 'Clashing Agendas: Inside the Welfare Trap' is the source for much of this chapter.

3. David Freud. (2021). Clashing Agendas; Inside the Welfare Trap. Nine Elms Books. Page 110.

4. Department for Work and Pensions. 21st Century Welfare. July 2010. Page 34.

5. Suzanne Heywood. (2021). What does Jeremy Think? Jeremy Heywood and the Making of Modern Britain. William Collins. Page 319.

6. Simon Walters and Brendan Carlin. Revealed: The blazing row between Iain Duncan Smith and George Osborne…and the tough-talking woman at the centre of it. Daily Mail and Mail on Sunday. August 22 2010.

7. David Freud. (2021). Clashing Agendas; Inside the Welfare Trap. Nine Elms Books. Page 158.

8. Martha Lane Fox. Directgov 2010 and beyond: Revolution not Evolution. October 2010.

9. David Freud. (2021). Clashing Agendas; Inside the Welfare Trap. Nine Elms Books. Page 181.

10. David Freud. (2021). Clashing Agendas; Inside the Welfare Trap. Nine Elms Books. Page 186.

11. David Freud. (2021). Clashing Agendas; Inside the Welfare Trap. Nine Elms Books. Page 187.

12. David Freud. (2021). Clashing Agendas; Inside the Welfare Trap. Nine Elms Books. Page 202.

13. David Freud. (2021). Clashing Agendas; Inside the Welfare Trap. Nine Elms Books. Page 211.

14. David Freud. (2021). Clashing Agendas; Inside the Welfare Trap. Nine Elms Books. Page 273.

15. David Freud. (2021). Clashing Agendas; Inside the Welfare Trap. Nine Elms Books. Page 230.

16. David Freud. (2021). Clashing Agendas; Inside the Welfare Trap. Nine Elms Books. Page 81.

17. Department for Work and Pension. Getting Britain Working: The Secretary of State for Work and Pensions Liz Kendall delivered a landmark speech setting out how Britain's system of employment support must be fundamentally reformed. July 23 2024. https://www. gov.uk/government/speeches/getting-britain-working

CHAPTER 6

1. House of Commons: Energy and Climate Change Committee. Oral evidence: Progress of smart meter roll-out. 16 December 2014.

2. Institute for Government. Explainer. Select Committees. May 2019. https://www.instituteforgovernment.org.uk/explainer/select-committees

3. Department of Trade and Industry. Meeting the Energy Challenge: A White Paper on Energy. May 2007.

4. Department of Energy and Climate Change. Smart Metering Implementation Programme: Prospectus.27 July 2010, Page 36.

5. The complexity of Crossrail's signalling challenge is explained well in: London Assembly. Transport Committee. April 2019. Derailed: Getting Crossrail back on track. Page 38.

6. Department of Energy and Climate Change. Towards a Smarter Future: Government response to the consultation on electricity and gas smart metering. December 2009. Page 10.

7. Department of Energy and Climate Change. Towards a Smarter Future: Government response to the consultation on electricity and gas smart metering. December 2009. Page 10.

8. National Audit Office. Delivery Environment Complexity Analytic (DECA): Understanding challenges in delivering project objectives. November 2022.

9. Infrastructure and Projects Authority. Project Routemap: Setting up projects for success. Updated 28 February 2022. https://www.gov.uk/ government/publications/improving-infrastructure-delivery-project-initiation-routemap

CHAPTER 7

1. Tim Burt. GEC wins £2bn submarine contract. Financial Times. 18 March 1997.

2. The 2011 report 'Lessons from the United Kingdom's Astute Submarine Program' commissioned from the National Defence Research Institute is the source for much of this chapter. RAND, National Defence Research Institute. Learning from Experience. Volume III. Lessons from the United Kingdom's Astute Submarine Program.

3. Peter Hennessy and James Jinks. The Silent Deep: The Royal Navy Submarine Service Since 1945. Penguin Books. 2015. Page 615.

4. Peter Levene. Send for Levene. Nine Elm Books. 2018. Page 42.

5. Peter Levene. Send for Levene. Nine Elm Books. 2018. Page 88.

6. Peter Hennessy and James Jinks. The Silent Deep: The Royal Navy Submarine Service Since 1945. Penguin Books. 2015. Page 617.

7. Peter Hennessy and James Jinks. The Silent Deep: The Royal Navy Submarine Service Since 1945. Penguin Books. 2015. Page 12.

8. Lucy Fisher and Sylvia Pfeifer. UK submarines hit by 'underfunding', warns former First Sea Lord. Financial Times. 6 August 2024.

CHAPTER 8

1. Gov.uk. What is the Magnox Swarf Storage Silo? https://www.gov.uk/government/case-studies/what-is-the-magnox-swarf-storage-silo

2. National Audit Office. The Nuclear Decommissioning Authority: Taking forward decommissioning. 2008.

3. Department for Trade and Industry. Managing the Nuclear Legacy: A strategy for action. 2002.

4. The Nuclear Installations Inspectorate became part of a new Office of Nuclear Regulation, ONR, in 2011.

5. National Audit Office. Managing risk reduction at Sellafield. 2012.

6. Martin Robinson. Nuclear plant bosses forced to pay back inappropriate expense claims including a £714 taxi bill for a CAT. *Daily Mail*. 9 September 2013.

7. Royal United Services Institute. Outsourcing Defence Procurement Remains High Risk Option. 30 July 2012. https://www.rusi.org/publication/outsourcing-defence-procurement-remains-high-risk-option

CHAPTER 9

1. Chapter 11 of Richard Bacon and Christopher Hope's book *Conundrum: Why Every Government Gets Things Wrong – And What We Can Do About It* is the source for much of this chapter.

2. Oliver Campion-Awwad, Alexander Hayton, Leila Smith and Mark Vuaran. The National Programme for IT in the NHS: A Case History. MPhil Public Policy. University of Cambridge. February 2014.

3. HM Treasury. The Wanless Report. Securing our Future Health: Taking a Long-Term View. April 2022. https://web.archive.org/web/20071003045037/http://www.hm-treasury.gov.uk/Consultations_and_Legislation/wanless/consult_wanless_final.cfm

4. Department of Health. Delivering 21st Century IT Support for the NHS: National Strategic Programme. 2002.

5. Richard Bacon and Christopher Hope. Conundrum: Why Every Government Gets Things Wrong – And What We Can Do About It. Biteback Publishing. 2013. Pages 176 and 239.

6. House of Commons. Committee of Public Accounts. Department of Health: The National Programme. for IT in the NHS. Report, together with formal minutes, oral and written evidence. 26 March 2007.

7. Richard Bacon and Christopher Hope. Conundrum: Why Every Government Gets Things Wrong – And What We Can Do About It. Biteback Publishing. 2013. Page 180.

8. National Audit Office. The National Programme for IT in the NHS. 2006. Page 53.

9. House of Commons. Committee of Public Accounts. Department of Health: The National Programme for IT in the NHS Twentieth Report of Session 2006–07. 26 March 2007.

10. Richard Bacon and Christopher Hope. Conundrum: Why Every Government Gets Things Wrong – And What We Can Do About It. Biteback Publishing. 2013. Page 183.

11. Richard Bacon and Christopher Hope. Conundrum: Why Every Government Gets Things Wrong – And What We Can Do About It. Biteback Publishing. 2013. Page 183.

12. Richard Bacon and Christopher Hope. Conundrum: Why Every Government Gets Things Wrong – And What We Can Do About It. Biteback Publishing. 2013. Page 187.

13. Richard Bacon and Christopher Hope. Conundrum: Why Every Government Gets Things Wrong – And What We Can Do About It. Biteback Publishing. 2013. Pages 190, 192 and 198.

14. Richard Bacon and Christopher Hope. Conundrum: Why Every Government Gets Things Wrong – And What We Can Do About It. Biteback Publishing. 2013. Page 187.

15. Richard Bacon and Christopher Hope. Conundrum: Why Every Government Gets Things Wrong – And What We Can Do About It. Biteback Publishing. 2013. Page 188.

16. Richard Bacon and Christopher Hope. Conundrum: Why Every Government Gets Things Wrong – And What We Can Do About It. Biteback Publishing. 2013. Page 196.

17. Jamie Doward. Chaos as £13bn NHS computer system falters. The Guardian. 10 August 2018. https://www.theguardian.com/society/2008/aug/10/nhs.computersystem

18. Hansard. House of Commons Debates. NHS IT Programme. 7 December 2009. https://publications.parliament.uk/pa/cm200910/cmhansrd/cm091207/debtext/91207-0004.htm

19. Department of Health. Press Release. The future of the National Programme for IT. 9 September 2010. https://webarchive.nationalarchives.gov.uk/ukgwa/20120503092804/http://www.dh.gov.uk/en/MediaCentre/Pressreleases/DH_119293

20. The Rt Hon. Professor the Lord Darzi of Denham. Independent Investigation of the National Health Service in England. September 2024. Page 103. https://assets.publishing.service.gov.uk/media/66f42ae630536cb92748271f/Lord-Darzi-Independent-Investigation-of-the-National-Health-Service-in-England-Updated-25-September.pdf

CHAPTER 10

1. Matthew Beard. Olympics head quit because of 'politics'. The Independent. 01 November 2006.

CHAPTER 11

1. Isabel Vogel for the UK Department of International Development. Review of the use of 'Theory of Change' in international development. Review Report. April 2012. https://www.theoryofchange.org/pdf/DFID_ToC_Review_VogelV7.pdf

2. Isabel Vogel for the UK Department of International Development. Review of the use of 'Theory of Change' in international development. Review Report. April 2012. Page 14.

3. Independent Commission for Aid Impact Report: UK aid under pressure: a synthesis of ICAI findings from 2019 to 2023. 13 Sep 2023. https://icai.independent.gov.uk/html-version/uk-aid-under-pressure/

CHAPTER 12

1. The Fulton Committee. The Civil Service. Volume. 1. Report of the Committee. Chairman: Lord Fulton. June 1968. Page 12. https://www.civilservant.org.uk/library/fulton/fulton1.pdf

2. Jason Groves and Matt Chorley. Blame game begins over benefits shake-up: IDS accuses civil servants of ignoring warning signs about Universal Credit plan. Daily Mail. 4 September 2013.

3. Prime Minister Rishi Sunak. Speech to the Conservative Party Conference. 4 October 2023.

4. Institute for Government. Who runs Whitehall? The background, appointment, management and pay of the civil service's top talent. May 2024. Page 4.

5. Institute for Government. Moving On: The costs of high staff turnover in the civil service. January 2019. Page 4. https://www.instituteforgovernment.org.uk/sites/default/files/publications/IfG_staff_turnover_WEB.pdf?form=MG0AV3

6. Prime Minister Rishi Sunak. Speech to the Conservative Party Conference. 4 October 2023.

7. Department for Transport. Press release. Transport Secretary announces urgent action to get a grip on spiralling HS2 costs. 20 October 2024. https://www.gov.uk/government/news/transport-secretary-announces-urgent-action-to-get-a-grip-on-spiralling-hs2-costs

CHAPTER 13

1. The NAO/OGC Common Causes of Project Failure were ubiquitous in the civil service twenty years ago. You now have to seek them out in obscure corners of the internet. http://miroslawdabrowski.com/

downloads/NAO%20OGC%20-%20Common%20causes%20of%20
project%20failure.pdf?form=MG0AV3

2. Civil Service Code. Updated 16 March 2015. https://www.gov.uk/
government/publications/civil-service-code/the-civil-service-code#fnref:1

3. Ministerial Code. Updated 6 November 2024. https://www.gov.uk/
government/publications/ministerial-code

4. Institute for Government. The updated guidance on the Osmotherly Rules:
Civil servants running the biggest projects will now be directly accountable
to Parliament. 20 October 2014. https://www.instituteforgovernment.org.uk/
article/comment/updated-guidance-osmotherly-rules#:~:text=The%2034-year-
old%20Osmotherly%20rules%2C%20providing%20guidance%20for%20
ministers,or%20SROs%29%20about%20the%20implementation%20of%20
key%20projects

5. Prime Minister David Cameron. Letter to Cabinet ministers. PM
Mandate for MPA. 25 January 2011. https://assets.publishing.service.gov.
uk/media/5a7ef45040f0b62305b8437e/PM_mandate_for_MPA_2011.pdf

6. Institute for Government. Power with purpose. Final report of the
Commission on the Centre of Government. March 2024. Page 102.

7. Lord Maude of Horsham. Independent Review of Governance and
Accountability in the Civil Service. November 2023. Page 22.

www.ingramcontent.com/pod-product-compliance
Lightning Source LLC
Chambersburg PA
CBHW071103280326
41928CB00051B/2801